A SEAFORD SKETCHBOOK

THE DRAWINGS OF HH EVANS 1849 - 1926

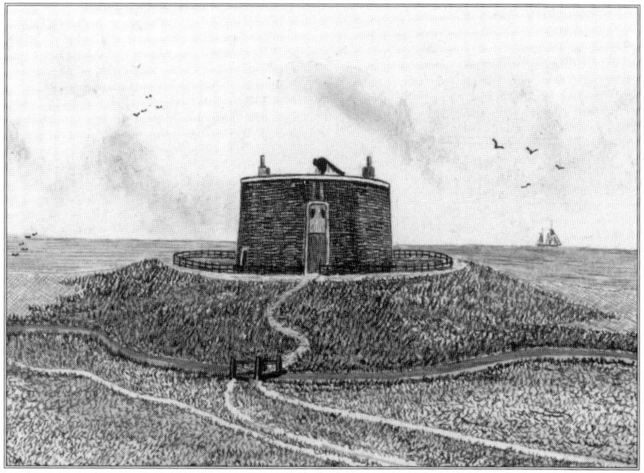

Researched and compiled by David Taylor and members of
The Seaford Museum and Heritage Society

S.B. Publications

First published in 2001 by S.B. Publications
19 Grove Road, Seaford, East Sussex BN25 1TP

ISBN 1 85770 235 2

Typeset and printed by Tansleys the Printers
19 Broad Street, Seaford, East Sussex BN25 1LS
Tel: 01323 891019 Fax: 01323 899484

Front cover: Seaford Beach looking west toward Newhaven, August 1882. The house at centre right is Telsemaure, the home of the Crook family who were well known local benefactors. The sea wall was completed in 1881.
(Size of original drawing 120 x 150mm).

Title page.: Martello Tower 74, the most westerly of a chain of defence protecting the English coast from the French. Built 1806-10 at a cost of £18,000 it housed 1 officer and 24 men.
(Size of original drawing 155x 210mm)

Back cover: St Leonard's Church showing lych gate, which was erected in 1896.
(Size of original drawing 150 x 105mm)

Contents

Acknowledgments

These drawings are taken primarily from the collection held by Seaford Museum and Heritage Society. The drawings on pages 4,15,17,47,48,49 and 50 are from the collection of Mrs A Davidson-Houston. The Museum wishes to thank Mrs Davidson-Houston and all the Museum Members who have contributed to the information given in the book. Special thanks go to Mrs Shelagh Houlton (nee Evans), great niece of HH Evans, for her assistance with the family history.

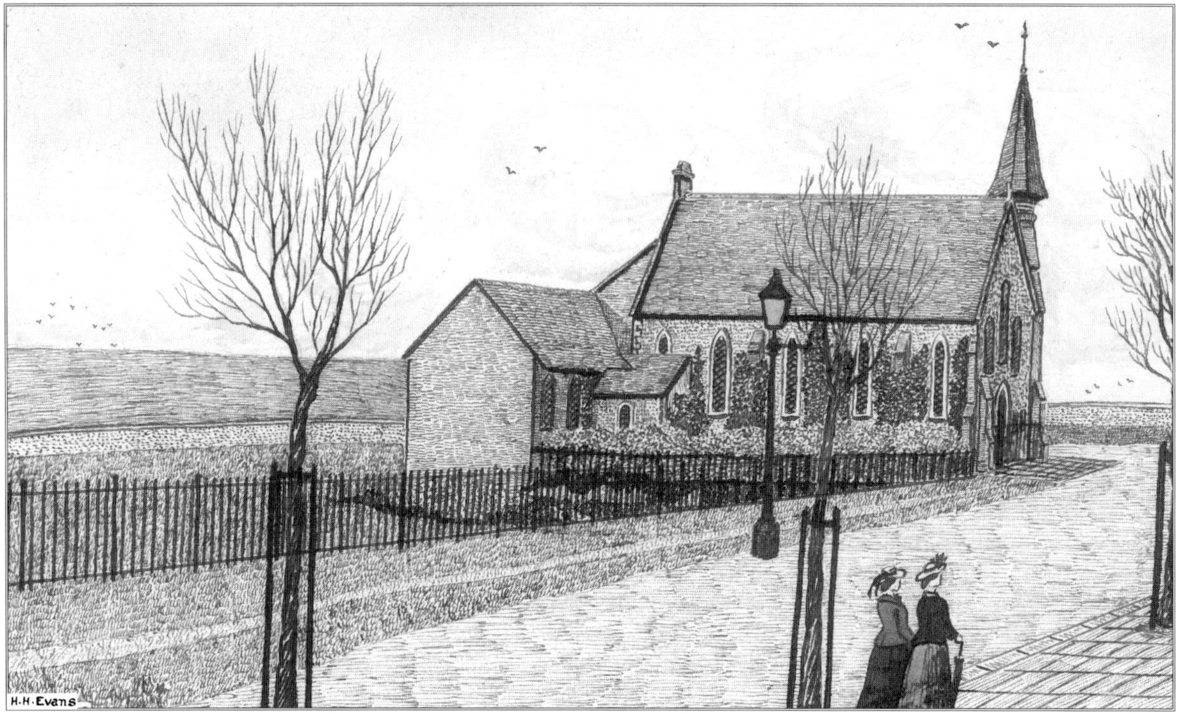

CONGREGATIONAL CHAPEL, *FROM* CLINTON PLACE *IN* 1881.
The foundation stone was laid by Mrs T. Crook, Decr 7th 1877.

Introduction

This volume presents a selection of the drawings of HH Evans, who appears to have spent the greater part of his life recording the events and buildings of Seaford and its surrounding areas, and documenting changes that occurred. Although frequently referred to as "Evans' Prints" these are not prints, all the drawings are originals, the only known reproductions from his time being a few postcards.

Harry Harison Evans' work is something of an enigma but some facts can be surmised from the examples of his work held by Seaford Museum and by other collectors; and the detective work continues.

His style of drawing changes very little over the years but his signature changes from H H Evans to HHE or H, but never "Wingy" or "Lumps" as he was known locally (due to the fact that he had only one arm).

The papers he used show no watermarks but vary from cheap drawing books to quality card. His method of working was to pin the paper to a drawing board and then use Indian ink and a mapping pen. A little wash was used for cloud, smoke or shadow but to our knowledge he never used colour. He occasionally used sepia ink.

He rarely dated the time at which he made his drawings but did date the event or time represented by the drawing. The earliest date represented in the collections to which we have access, is a view of Seaford Town in 1785. This is a copy of one of a set of six drawings by A Grimm (drawings now in the British Museum). He also copied drawings from The Illustrated London News, one of which was the great explosion of Seaford Head Cliff in 1850. Several drawings of the great flood and its aftermath were made by him, but whether these drawings are contemporary with the events or drawn retrospectively is a mystery. The flood occurred in 1875 when he was 26 years old but the only dated drawing of the flood was made in 1897. Like many of his compositions the drawing of Church Street at the time of the flood was taken from the work of J Moxon, a French artist working for The Illustrated London News.

Not only did he copy compositions from known artists, he also copied photographs taken by Mr W R Wynter, a well known local photographer and pharmacist and a friend of Evans' Father. W R Wynter was also a keen local historian, the author of "Old Seaford" published by Farncombe and Co in 1922, and used one of Evans' drawings as an illustration. The descriptions of events, written under the drawings in a fine, copperplate hand were not always correct and he repeated drawings of the same subject with differing details such as brick walls, flint walls and windows. Without dates we can never know which were the master drawings but it seems probable that he kept a collection of photographs and postcards to work from.

Many of his drawings survive as numbered collections, either in a drawing book or listed in special folders and it seems probable that he was commissioned to produce sets of drawings as gifts. This would also account for the repetition and slight differences in the drawings. At present we have located approximately 200 drawings, including one collection that had found its way to Canada and returned to Seaford in 1996. In January, 2001, a further collection of 50 drawings came to light (seven of which have been included in this book), which had originally been given to Mr Barwell, a Seaford solicitor by Miss Gertrude Danby, daughter of one of the last Bailiffs of the town and herself an eminent resident and councillor. We believe that there may be many other drawings in existence and hope to continue to record the work of this local artist.

Family Tree

Descendants of Rev. Thomas Evans

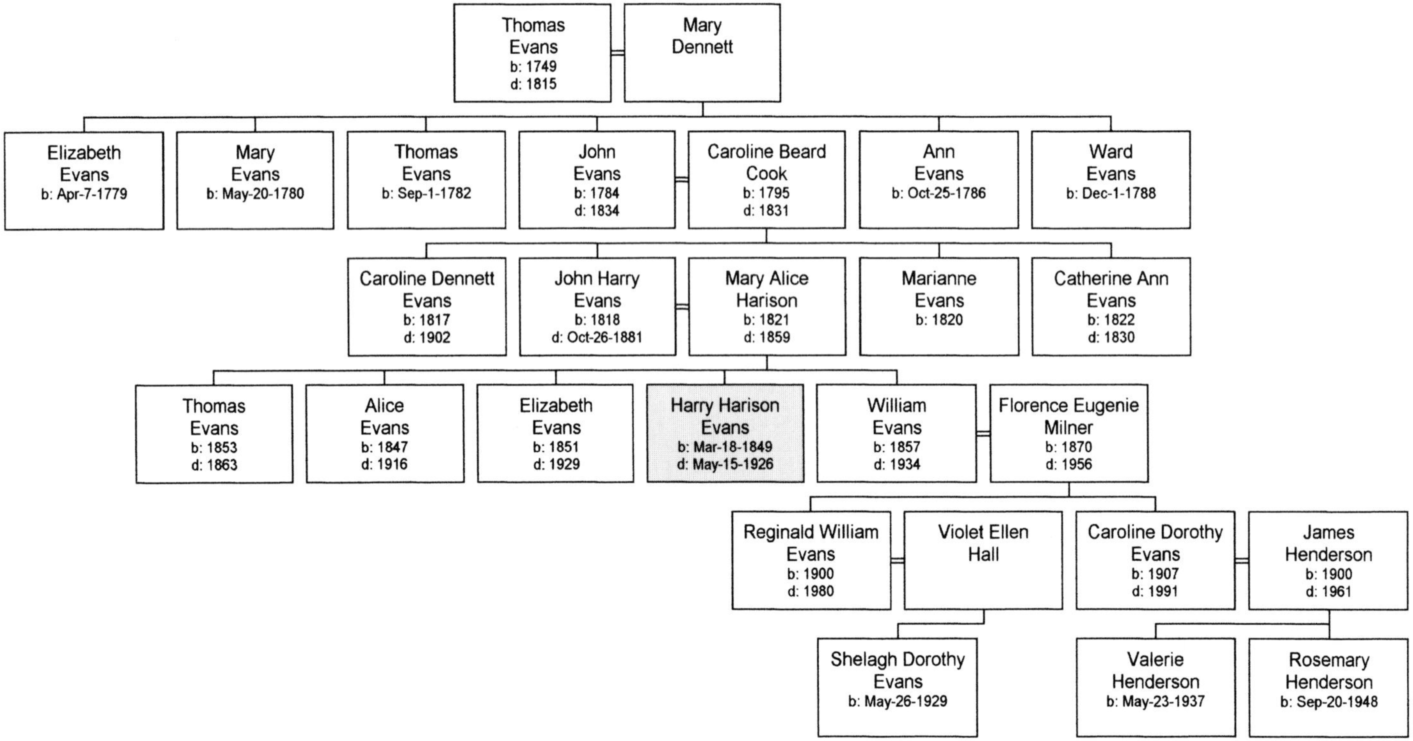

The Life of HH Evans

H H Evans was born in Seaford on 18th March 1849 and named Harry Harison Evans. His great grandfather had been the Rev. Thomas Evans, Vicar of St Leonard's Parish Church, Seaford and his father was John Harry Evans (MA.MB.Oxon. MRCS). a surgeon who was also a Jurat and Freeman of Seaford. HH Evans was the second of five children, of whom only the youngest, William, married. At the time of the 1851 census the family and their servants were living in High Street. As a leading citizen John Evans was a member of a committee to promote Seaford as a health resort (1858). Also on the committee were Dr Tyler Smith and Mr W R Wynter, the local chemist and photographer whose early photographs formed the basis for many of HH Evans' drawings. It is thought that John Evans may have known Charles Dickens through giving evidence to a public health committee. Harry Harison Evans was disabled, having only one arm, but when and how he lost his arm is unknown at present. There is a document that quotes his sister as saying, after his death, that he had lost his arm "some forty years ago". Once again there are many stories and many theories and the detective work goes on.

His mother died in 1859 in childbirth when the youngest surviving child was only two years old and in 1867 the family moved to 2 Pelham Place. The 1871 census shows HH Evans as 'office clerk, unemployed' but by 1881 the census shows Harry as living with his Aunt Caroline at 6 Clinton Place and does not list an occupation. It is possible that he lost his arm at some time between these two dates. The 1881 census also shows his father, who died in October of that year, as having retired to Steyne Cottages in South Street.

Evans seems to have lived in turn with various members of his family, at one time with his oldest sister, Alice at 'Meadowcroft' in East Street but he spent his latter years with his sister Elizabeth at 5 Hindover Road. Alice died in 1916 in Leigh-on-Sea and her death certificate describes her as "formerly a mission worker" but it is not known when she left Seaford. HH Evans died in May 1926 and his sister Elizabeth died at 2 Parkside Road in 1929. These members of the family are buried in Seaford Cemetery.

There are many myths surrounding Evans. One much repeated is that he could be found in The Plough public house with drinks lined up in front of him in payment for drawings that he dashed off. In view of the quality of most of the drawings this is not very credible. Evidence for his use of a drawing board comes from the pinholes to be found in the corners of many of his drawings. Also from one of the very few contemporary accounts given in a letter to George Jakens (a founder of Seaford Museum), in which Mr G Morling recalls "...seeing HHE at the gate of the Hindover Road house and also seeing him through the window, sitting at a table in the front room, drawing".

The Museum and Harry Harison Evans' surviving relatives hope eventually to fill the gaps in the life story of this still rather shadowy man, whose name is so well known.

Seaford Town Centre Map, 1872

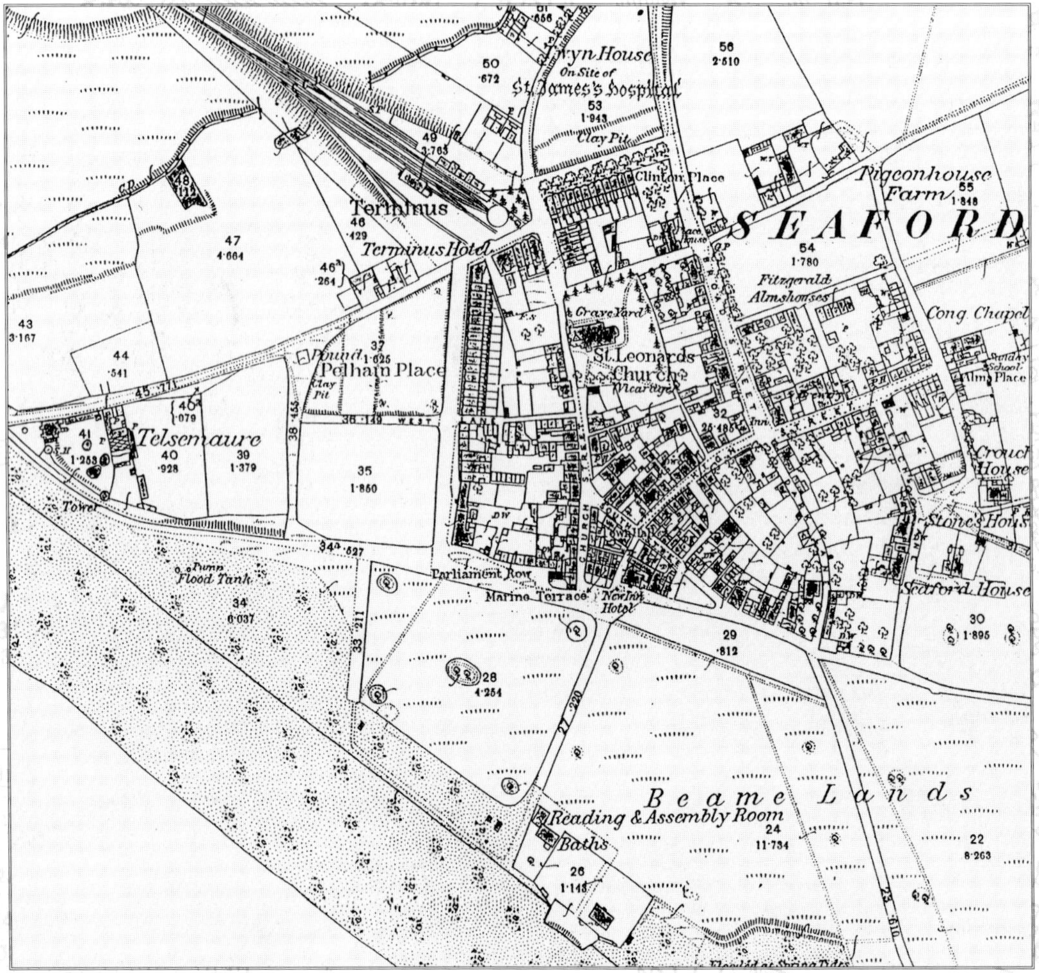

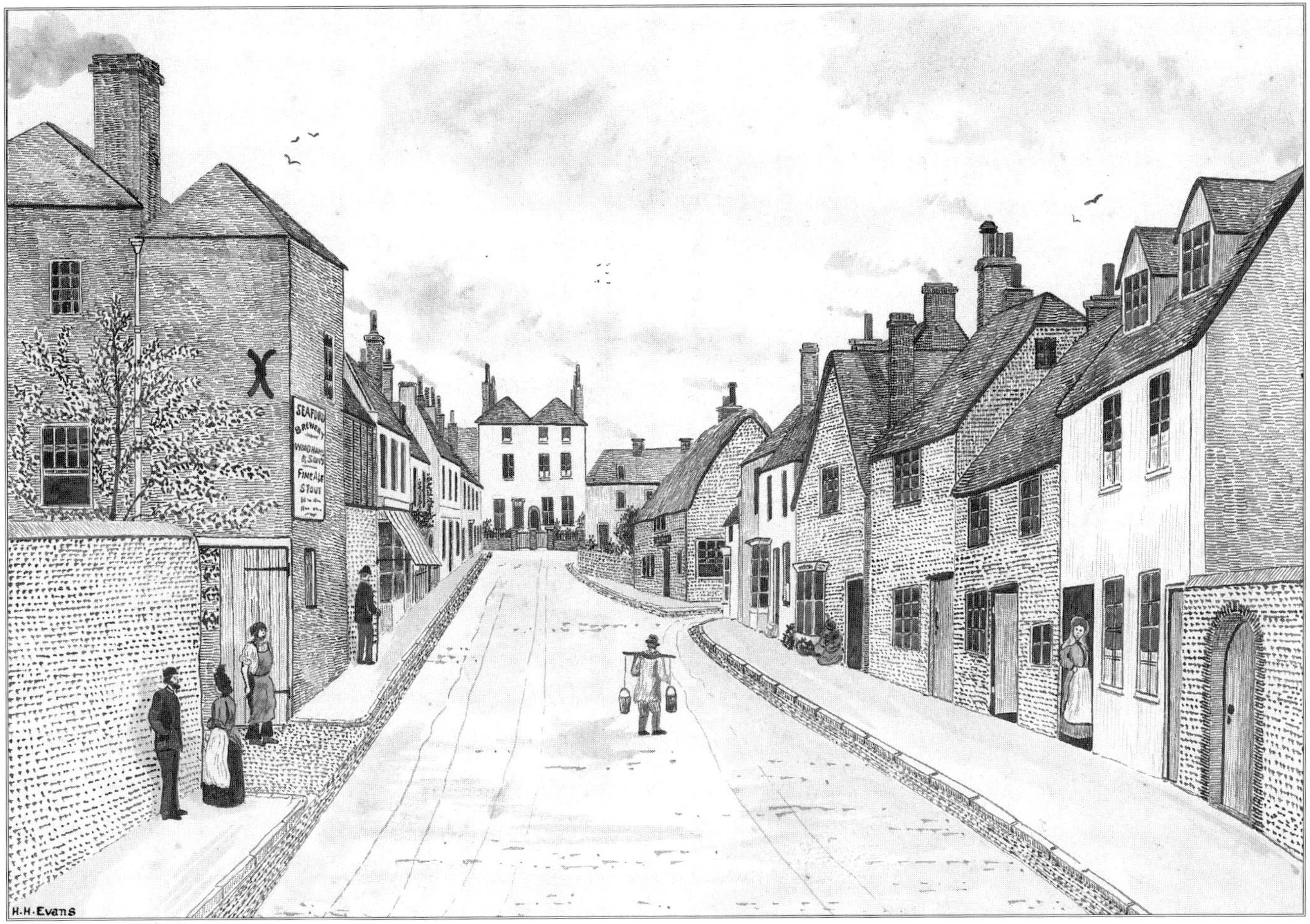

UPPER HIGH STREET 1870.
WOODHAMS' BREWERY ON THE LEFT HAND.

Looking up High Street from close to its junction with Broad Street. Left foreground shows rear of Old Tree Inn.
The old Police Station stood on the corner of Crouch Lane. (Size of original drawing 160 x 210mm)

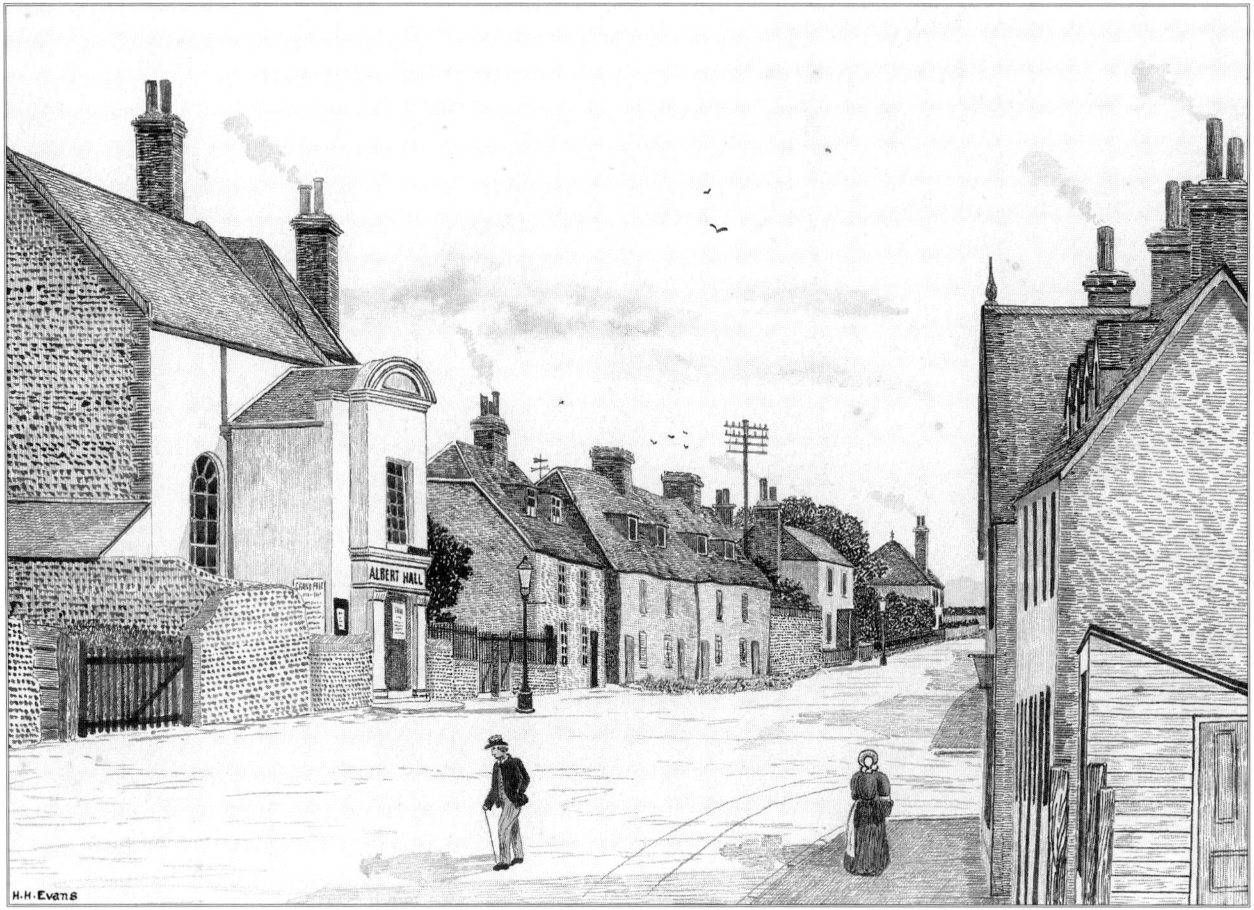

— OLD COTTAGES IN EAST STREET. —
— PULLED DOWN AS DANGEROUS IN 1905. —

Looking along East Street towards The Crouch, near the junction with High Street. The building on the left is the "Albert Hall", once a chapel and converted by Major Crook. Crouch House, seen in the distance, was once visited by General Gordon as a boy. Later it became the offices of Seaford Urban District Council. (Size of original drawing 160 x 210mm)

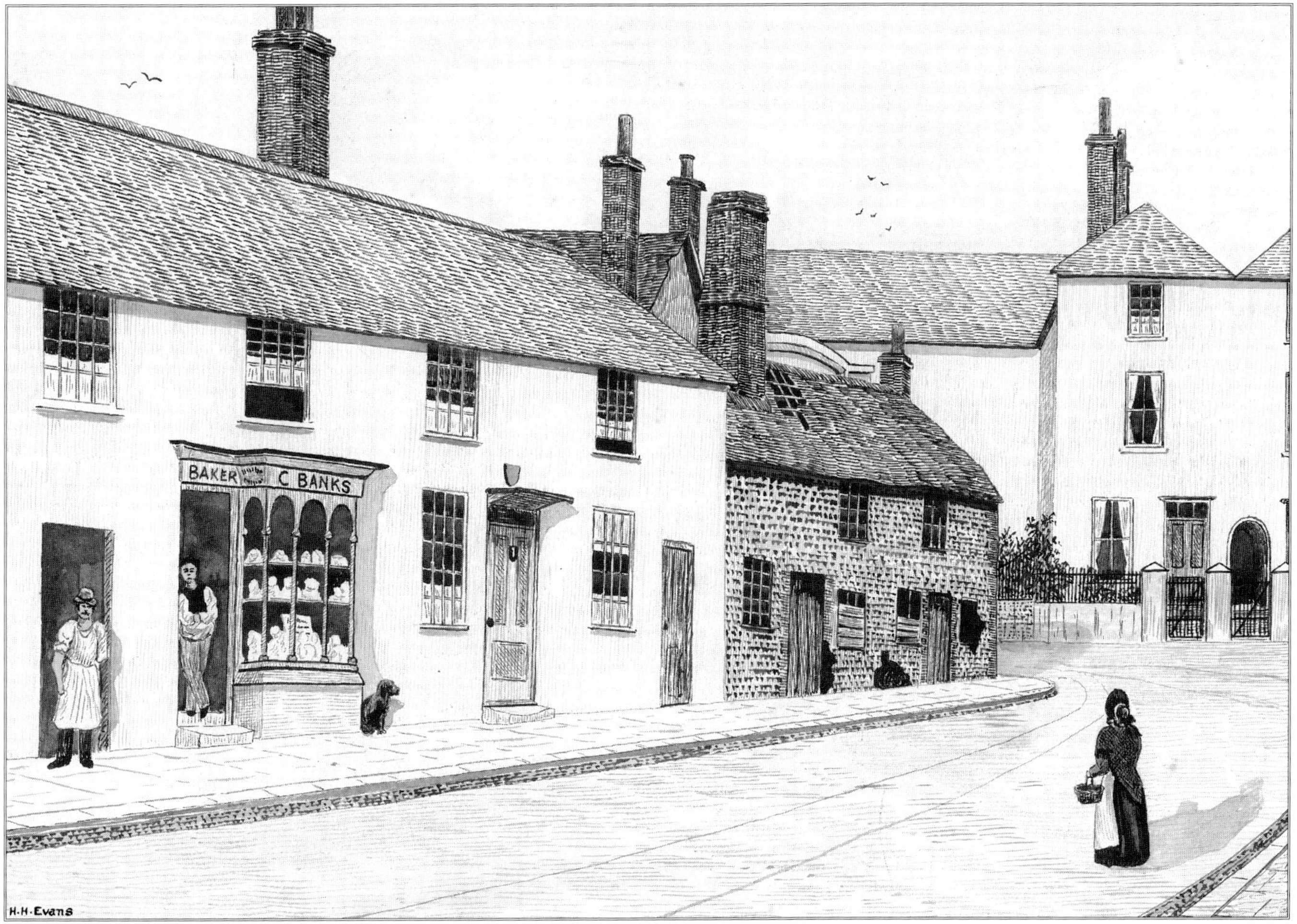

OLD COTTAGES AT THE TOP OF HIGH ST.
ASHLEY HOUSE BUILT ON SITE 1884.

Near the top of High Street, at its junction with East Street, with detail of cottages. (Size of original drawing 165 x 215mm)

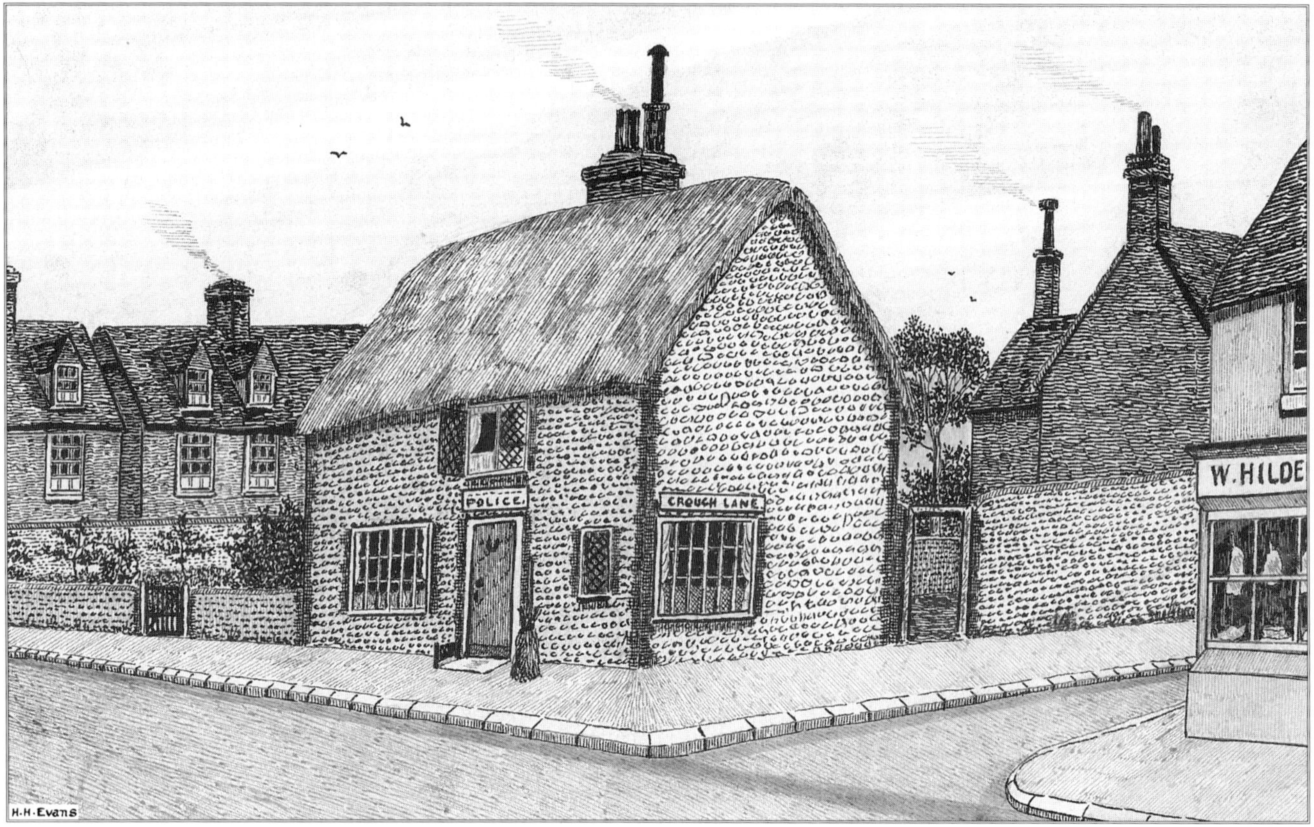

POLICE STATION, *IN HIGH STREET* 1864.

Penwatham Terrace is now built on this site, and on the opposite side of the street stood the "Rising Sun," now after alterations renamed the "Cinque Ports" Hotel.

Detail of the old Police Station on the corner of Crouch Lane. (Size of original drawing 160 x 180mm)

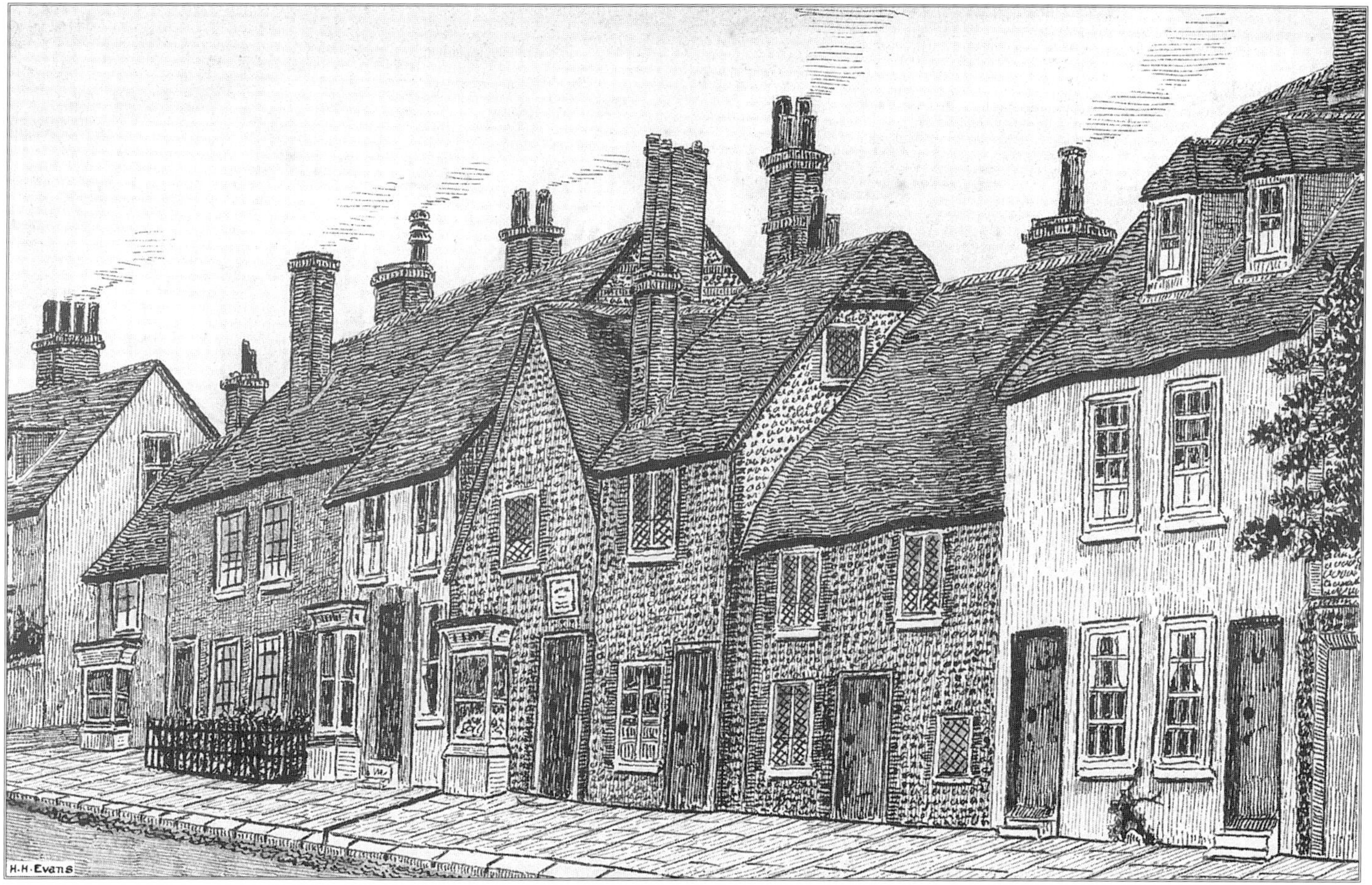

OLD COTTAGES IN HIGH STREET, SEAFORD.
Pulled down, and shops built in 1897.

Detail of houses in High Street 1897. Note that houses have replaced the old Police Station on the corner of Crouch Lane.
NB The next Police Station was built at the beginning of Chichester Road. (Size of original drawing 100 x 138mm)

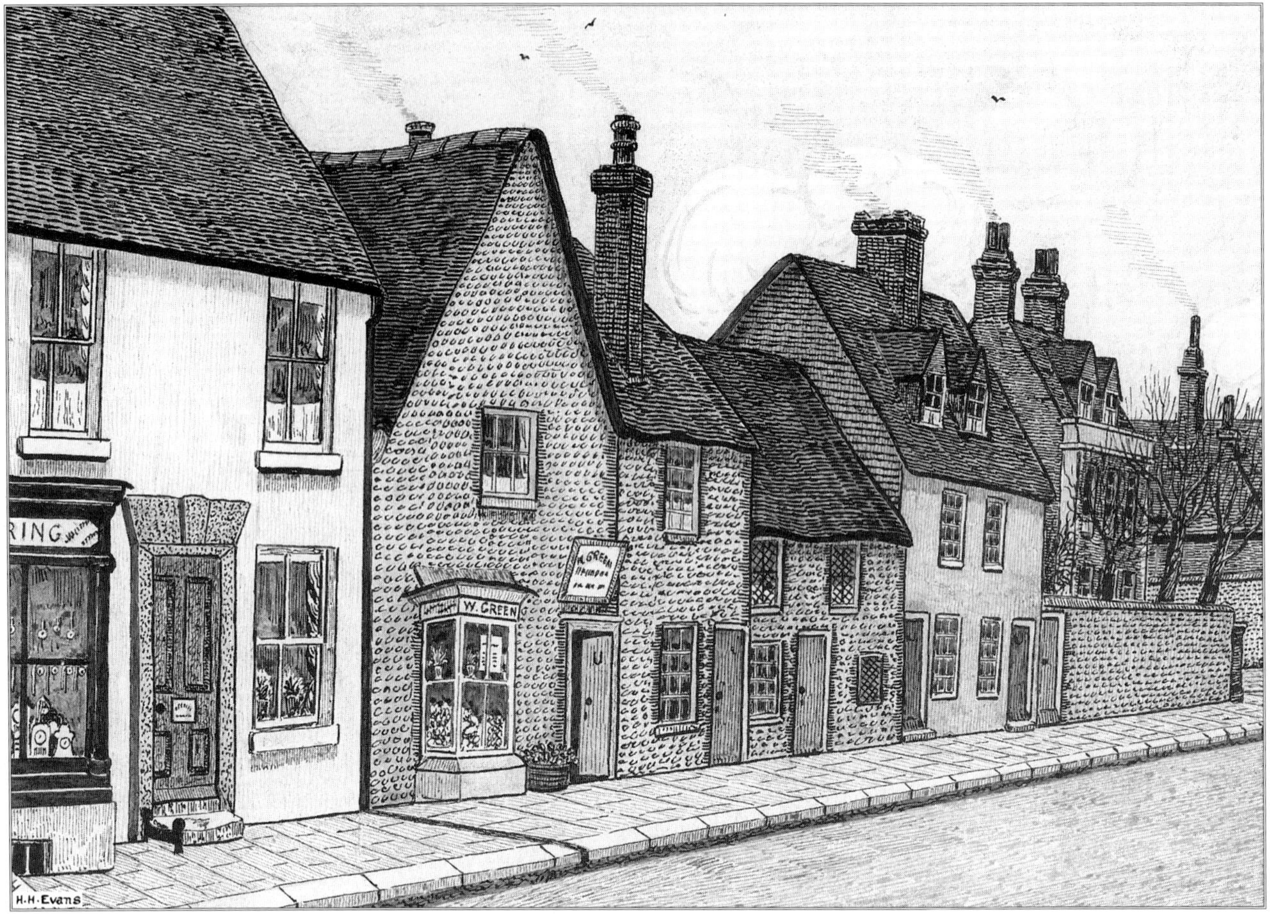

OLD COTTAGES IN HIGH STREET.

Pulled down, and the present shops built in 1897.

Detailed view of cottages in High Street taken from an early photograph. On the extreme right of the picture it is possible to see the junction with Saxon Lane. The house on the corner still stands with a shop front built on to it. (Size of original drawing 145 x 180mm)

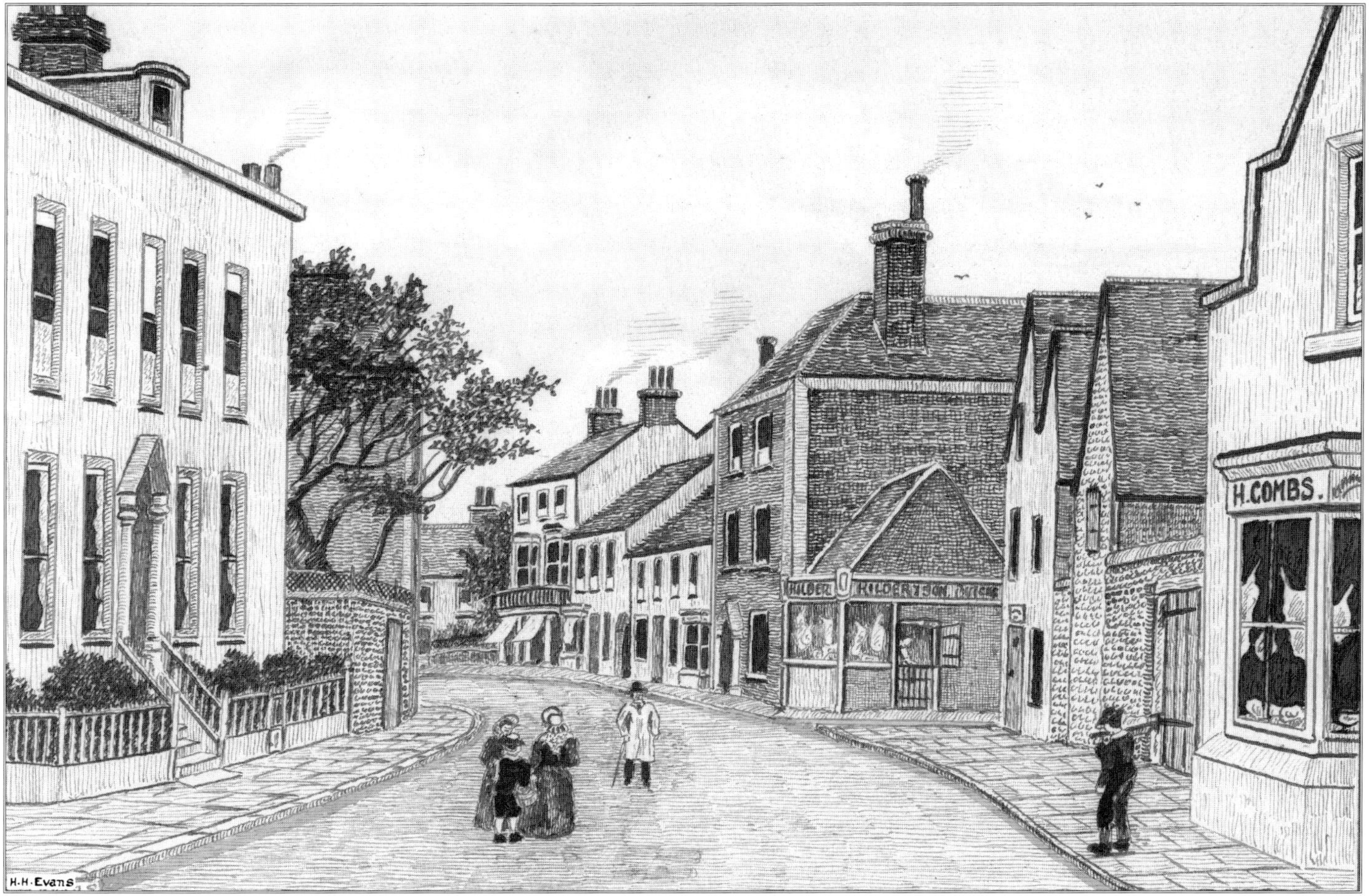

HIGH STREET 1880.
Looking S.

High Street looking south from the junction with Broad Street.
On the left is Talland House and on the right the entrance to Church Lane with the Old House beyond. (Size of original drawing 110 x 150mm)

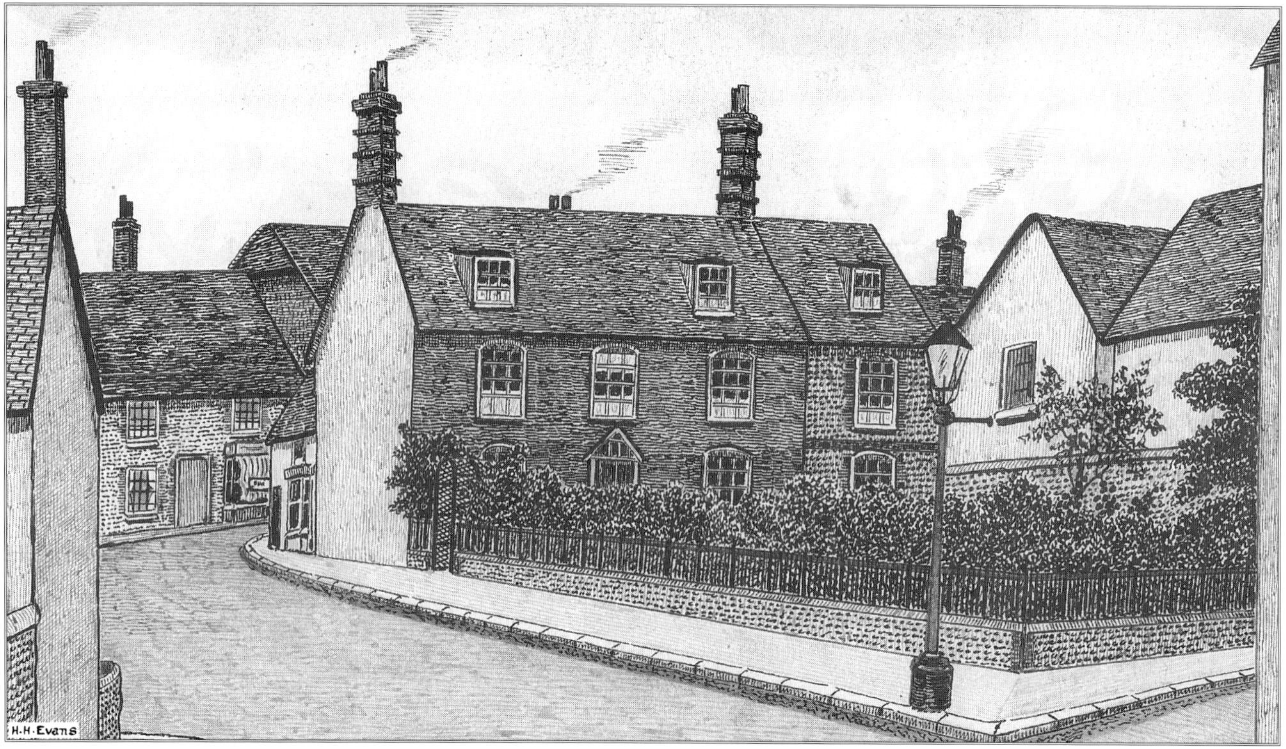

THE LAWN, *BOTTOM OF HIGH STREET*

A Baptist Chapel was built in this garden in 1887 and was in use as such until 1908 when the one in Broad Street was opened, it was soon after this altered into three lockup shops as at present time. A shop window has also been placed in the side of Lawn house.

The bottom end of High Street looking along South Street towards the bottom of Church Street.
The Old Town Hall would be out of sight to the left. (Size of original drawing 170 x 180mm)

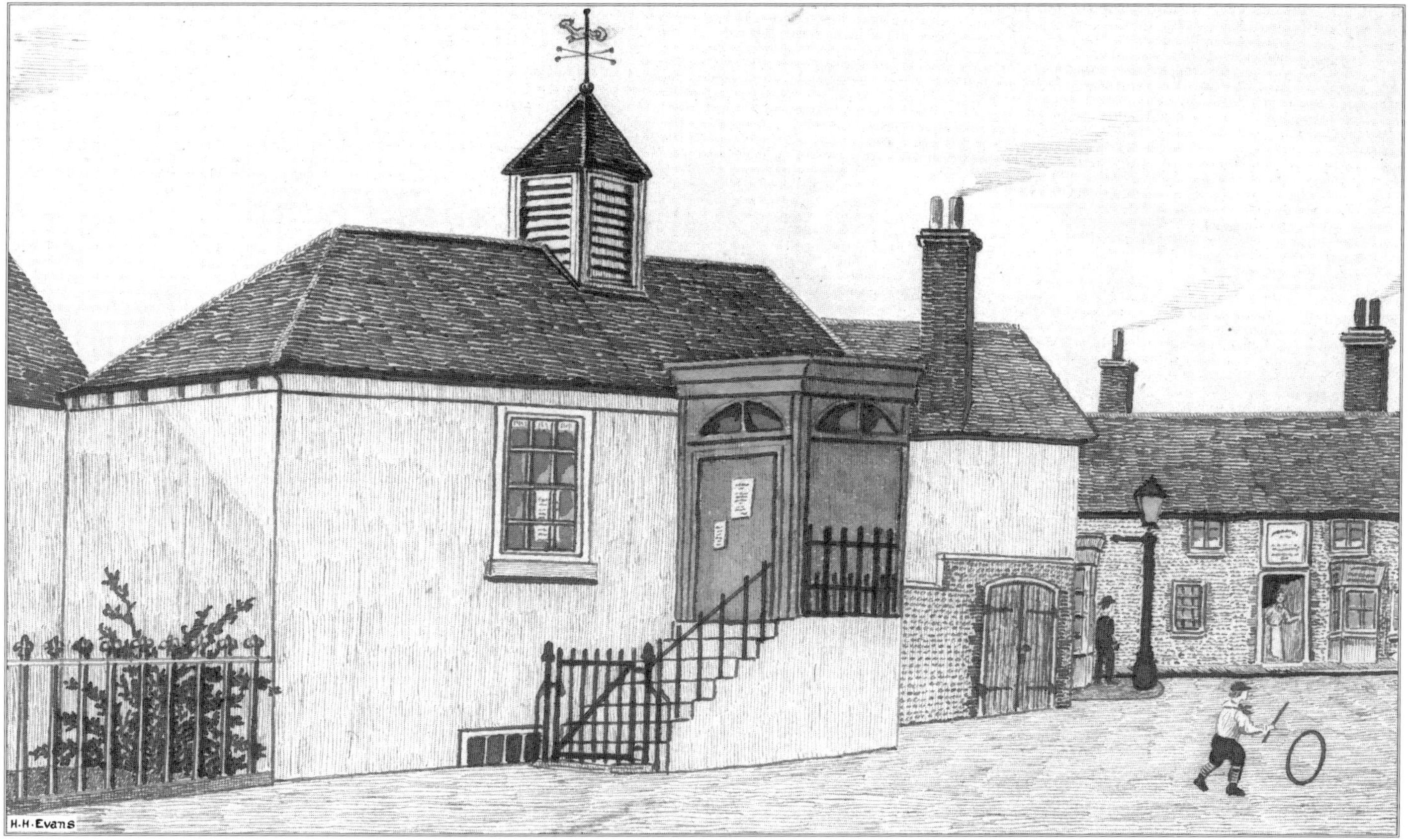

THE OLD TOWN HALL
NOW USED BY THE FIRE BRIGADE.

The first Corporation was in 1562 and lasted until the 25th March 1886 when the Corporation of Seaford came to an end by Act of Parliament. All Baliffs were elected here.

The Old Town Hall in South Street. The building still stands although the steps have been removed and public toilets have been built in what was the prisoners' exercise yard. (Size of original drawing 125 x 160mm)

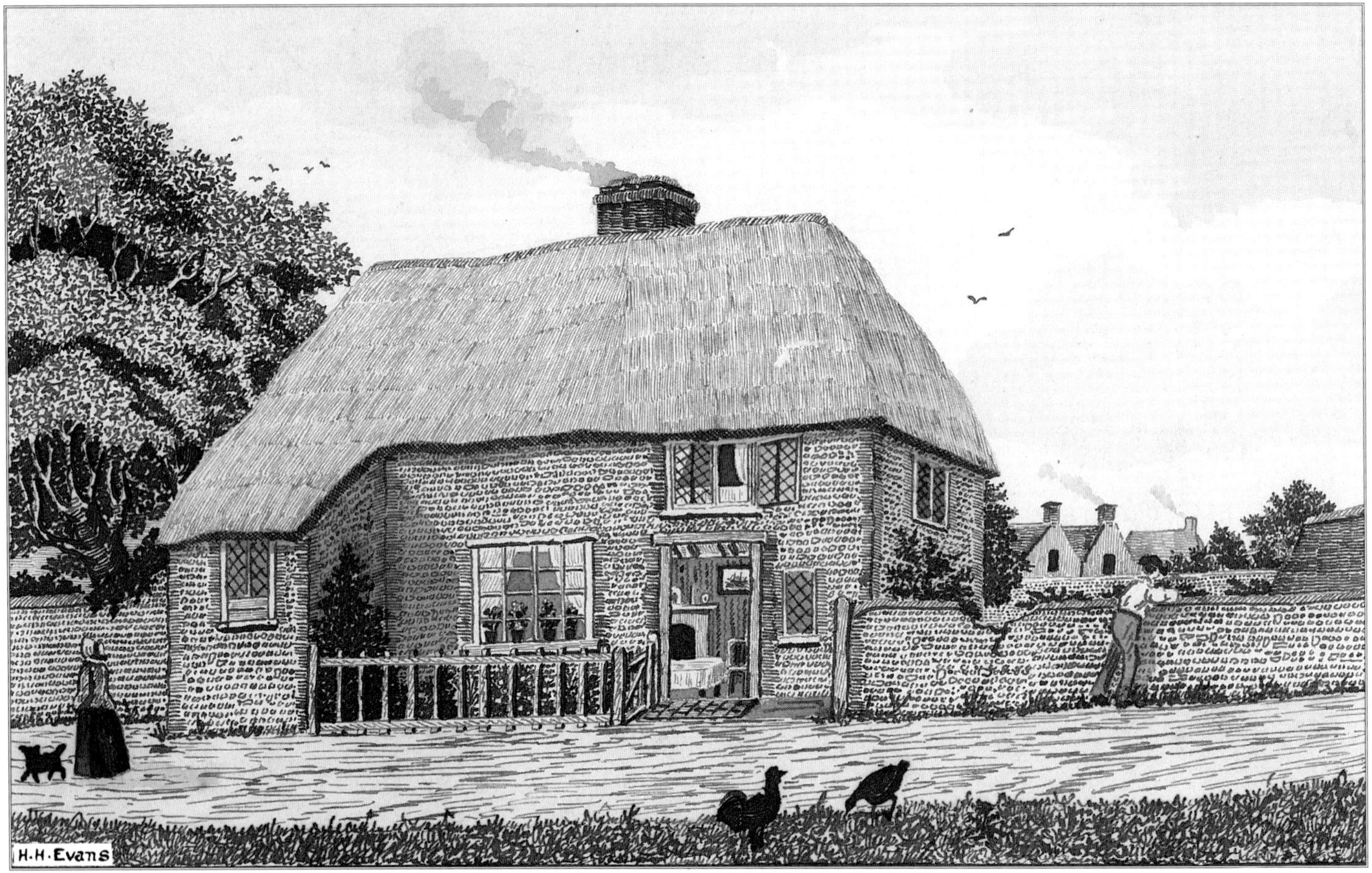

COTTAGE IN DARK {SAXON} LANE, SEAFORD
Pulled down, and two villas built

View of cottage in Saxon Lane that was later pulled down. Note the detail seen through the open door.
(Size of original drawing 120 x 175mm)

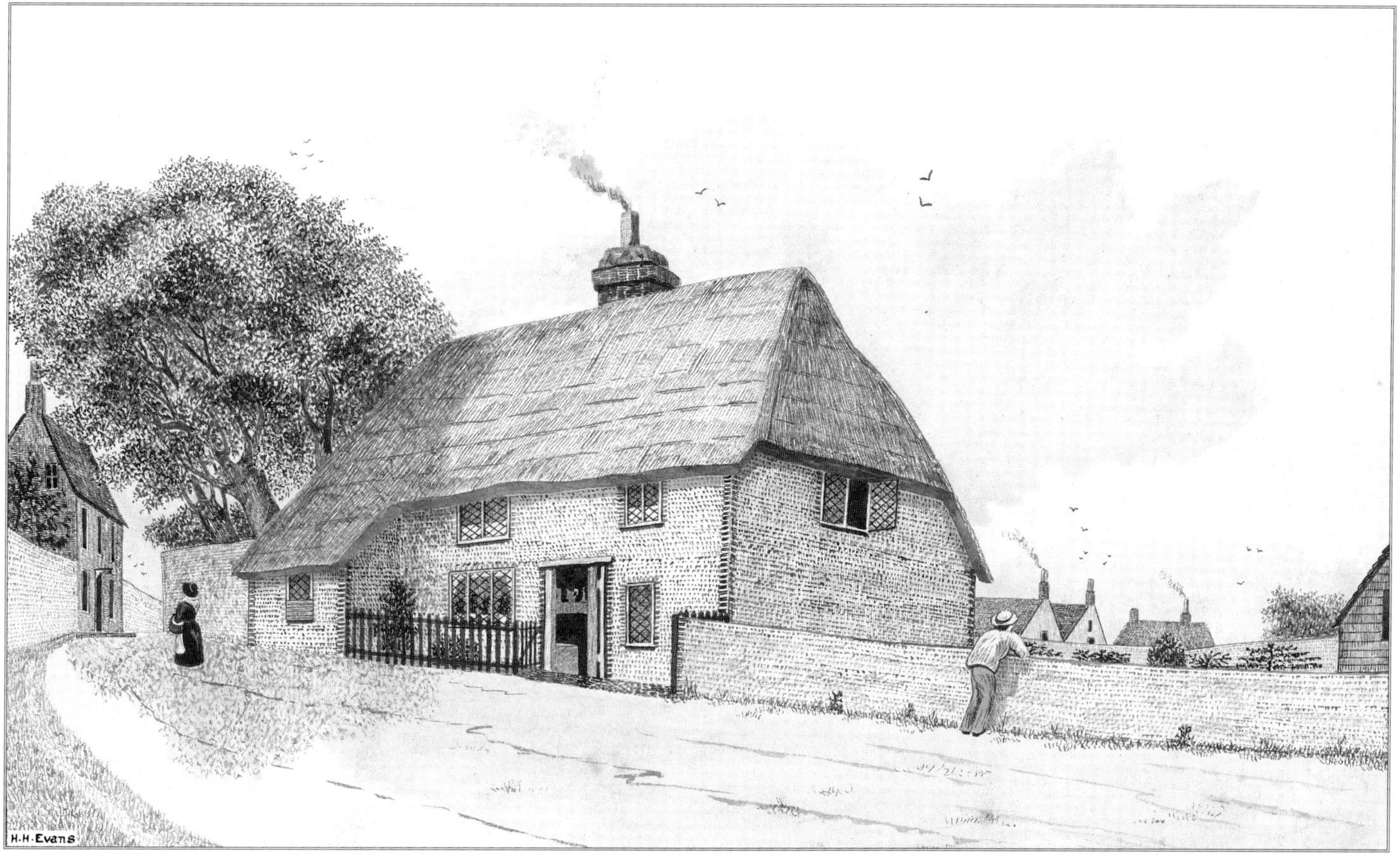

COTTAGE IN DARK LANE,

PULLED DOWN AND VILLAS BUILT ON SITE.

Another view of the cottage in Saxon Lane looking south and at the left of the picture showing the building, now known as Pear Tree Cottage, that still exists. NB The Pear Tree Cottage drawn by Evans and shown on page 35 stood in Church Street.

(Size of original drawing 190 x 290mm)

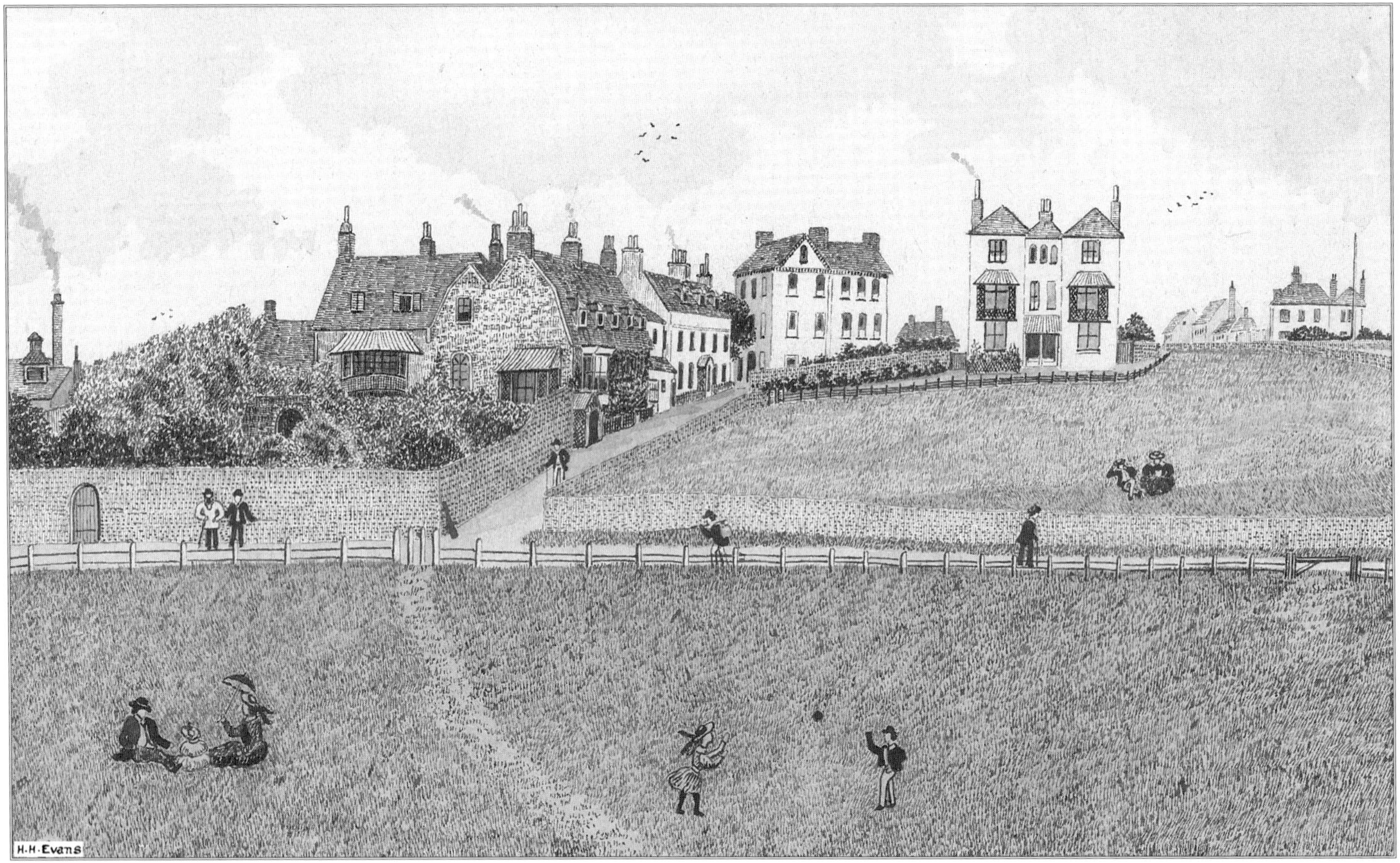

OLD SEAFORD HOUSE, *AND THE CROUCH.*

The Common looking towards The Crouch and end of East Street.
Stones House can be seen in the centre of the drawing and Seaford House and garden to the left.
(Size of original drawing 145 x 225mm)

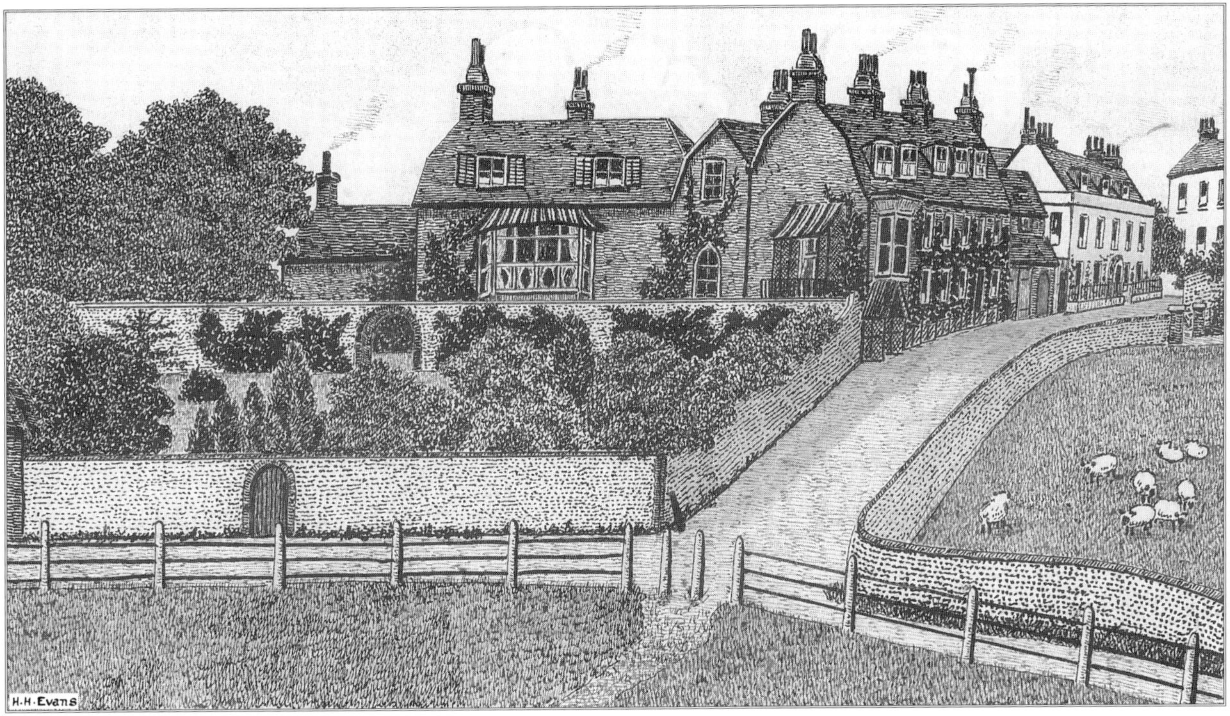

OLD SEAFORD HOUSE

From the Common.

It belonged to Lord Howard de Walden, Baron of Seaford, it was here that Lord Tennyson, who was a frequent visitor, wrote the funeral ode to the Duke of Wellington. Mr Geo Holland bought it 1860 and soon after had it pulled down, and the present one built.

Detailed view of old Seaford House. It once belonged to Lord Howard de Walden, Baron Seaford and Alfred Lord Tennyson was said to have written the funeral ode to the Duke of Wellington while staying there. The house was rebuilt in 1860 and that house was demolished to make way for the current building on the site. (Size of original drawing 170 x 180mm)

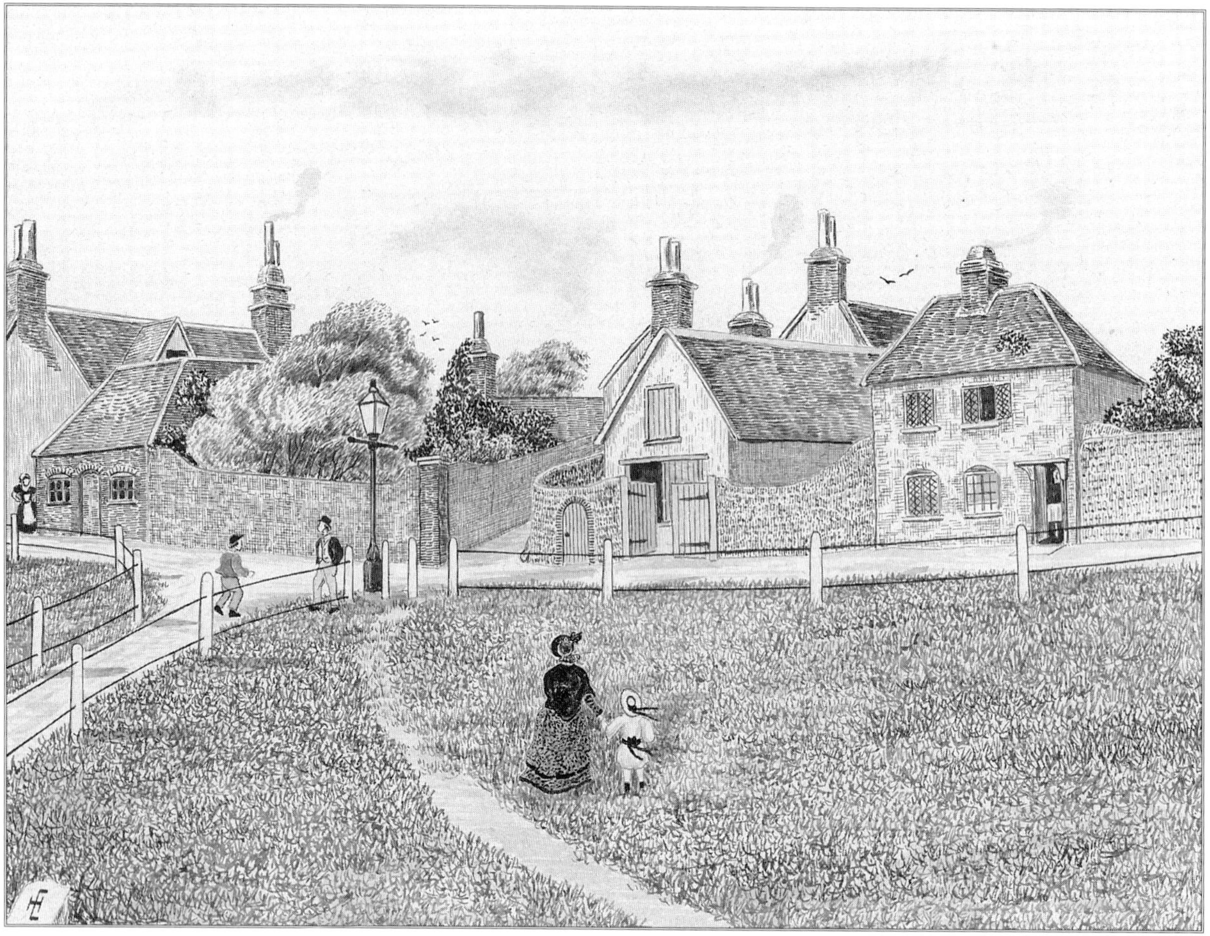

The corner of Steyne Road and end of Saxon Lane showing wall and gate into garden of Seaford House - now site of Barn Theatre.
(Size of original drawing 115 x 150mm)

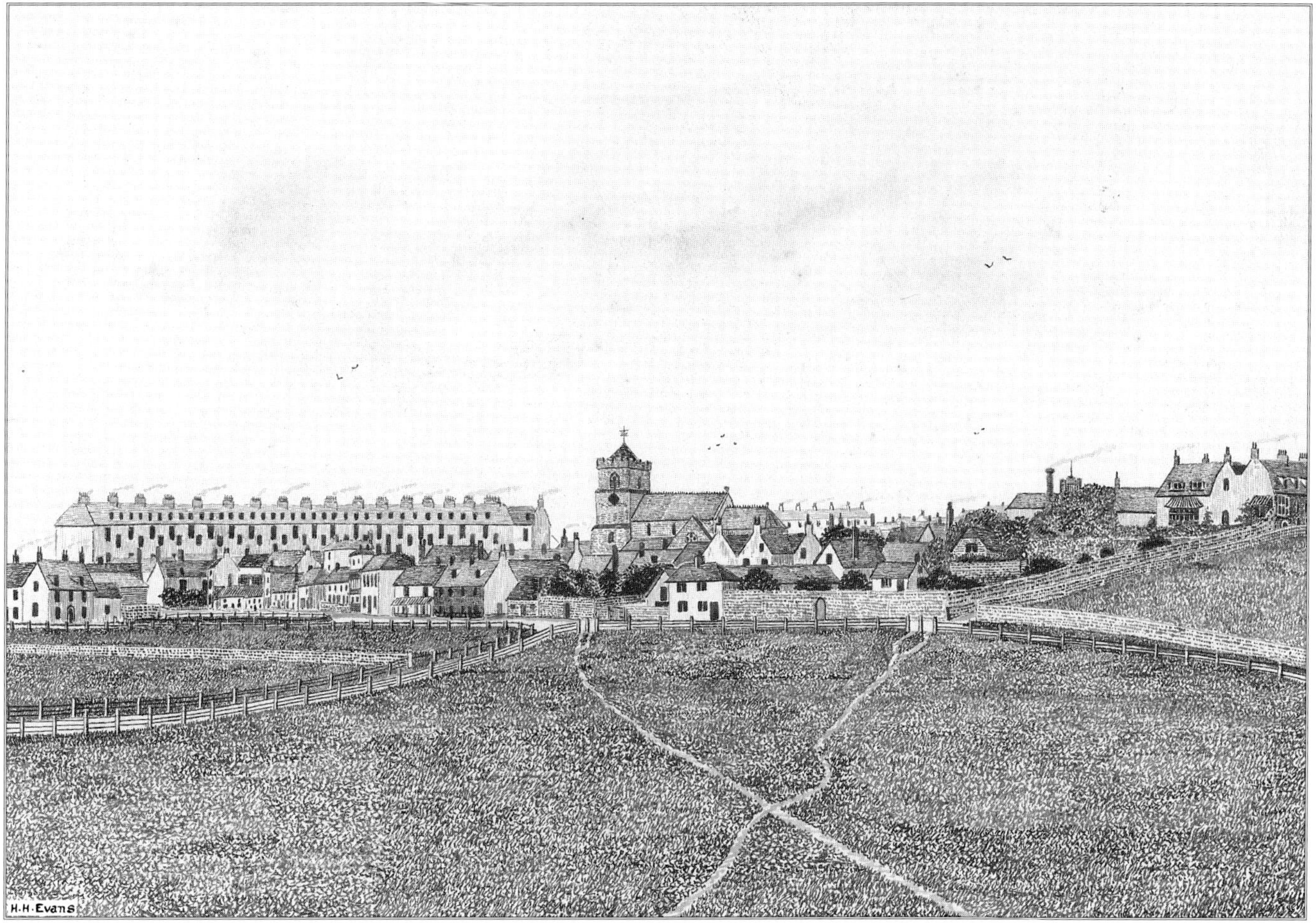

Seaford, Before the Flood 1875.

Seaford from the Common showing the line of the Steyne along the edge of the mediaeval harbour.
(Size of original drawing 170 x 180mm)

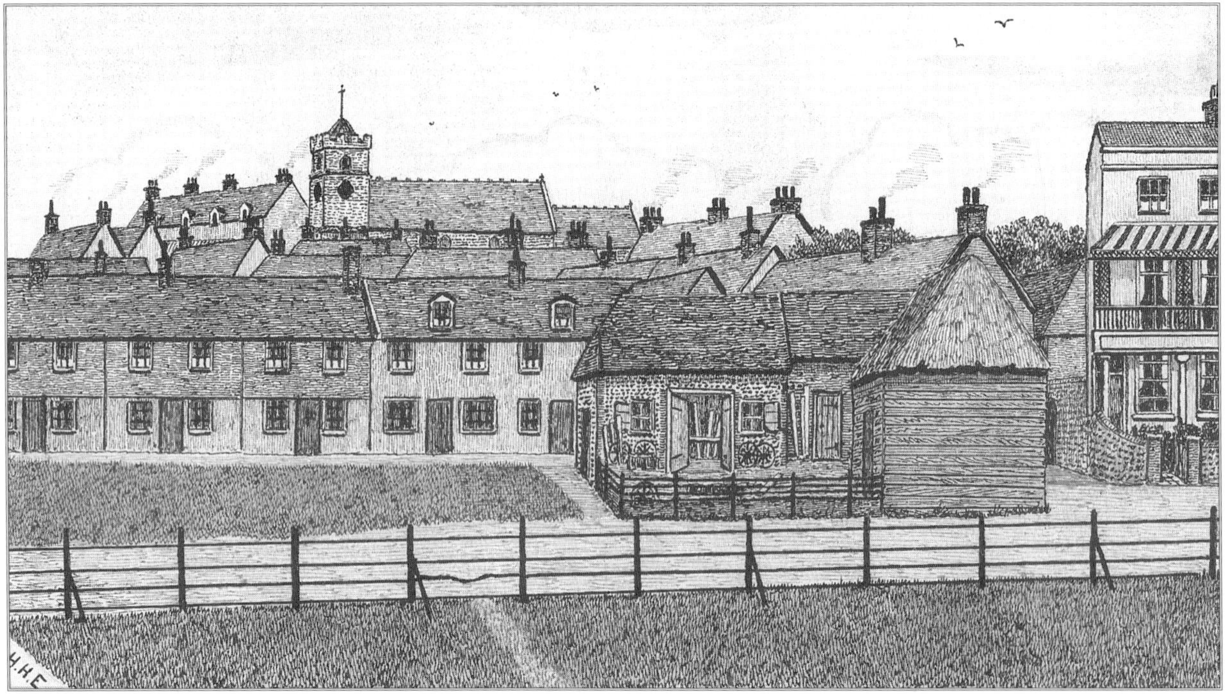

THE OLD WHEEL-WRIGHT'S SHOP & PARLIAMENT ROW.

Ockendens wheelwright shop, was completely washed down in the great sea flood of 1875. The cottages of Parliament row suffered considerable damage as well as the whole front of the town. The road in the foreground was then the only road to Newhaven &c. which went in front of Telsemaure and also Blatchington Battery.

The old Wheelwright's shop and Parliament Row. Parliament Row and Marine Terrace, seen on the right of the picture, are still in existence. The name of Parliament Row comes from the time when Seaford was a pocket borough and voters were housed there at the time of the elections. (Size of original drawing 172 x 180mm)

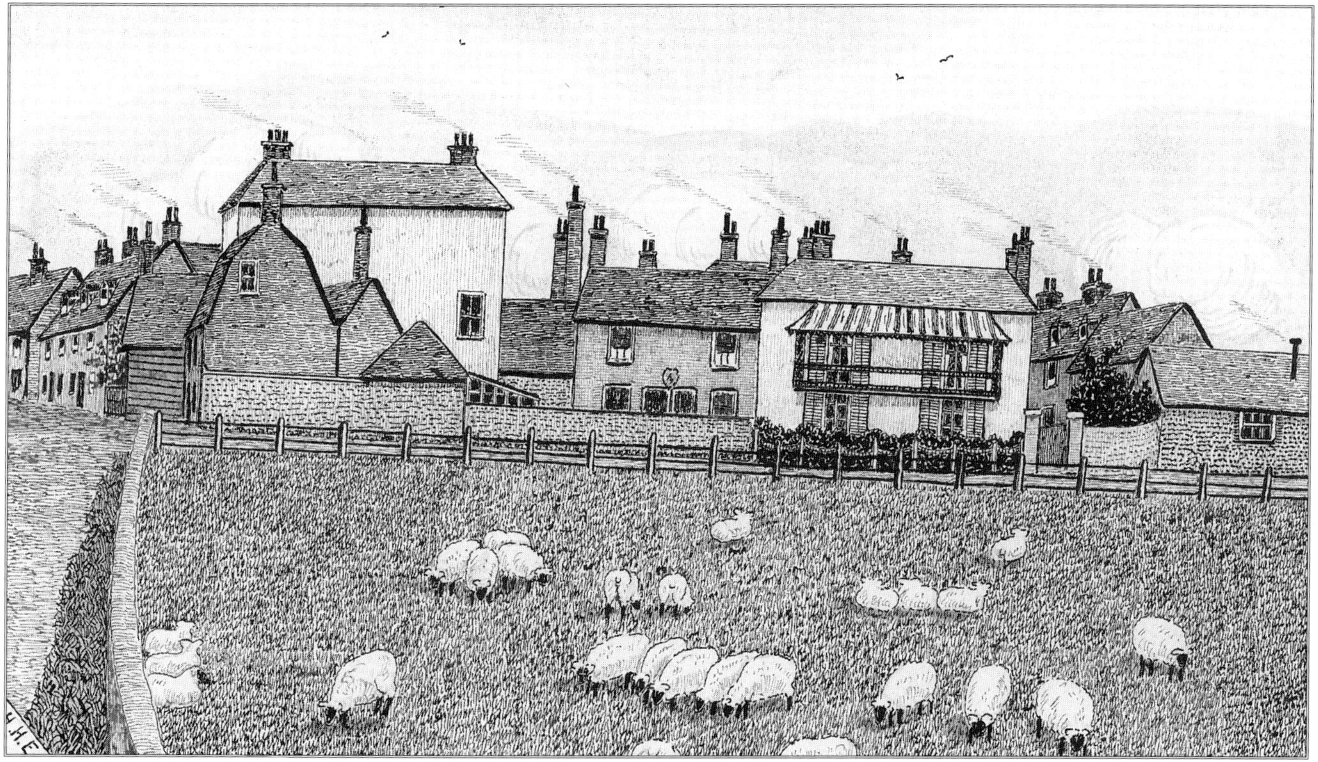

BAY HOUSE AND ANGEL COTTAGES.
SEAFORD.

Bay House was bought by Mr. Thos. Crook, in 1860, pulled down and the Bay Hotel built with coach house and stables extending to West lane, these were soon pulled down and the present extension made containing dining billiard and bedrooms with public bar &c. The field in front was used by Wood the butcher for cows & sheep grazing.

Looking east to Pelham Place from a field near to where it is crossed by West Street. (Size of original drawing 175 x 180mm)

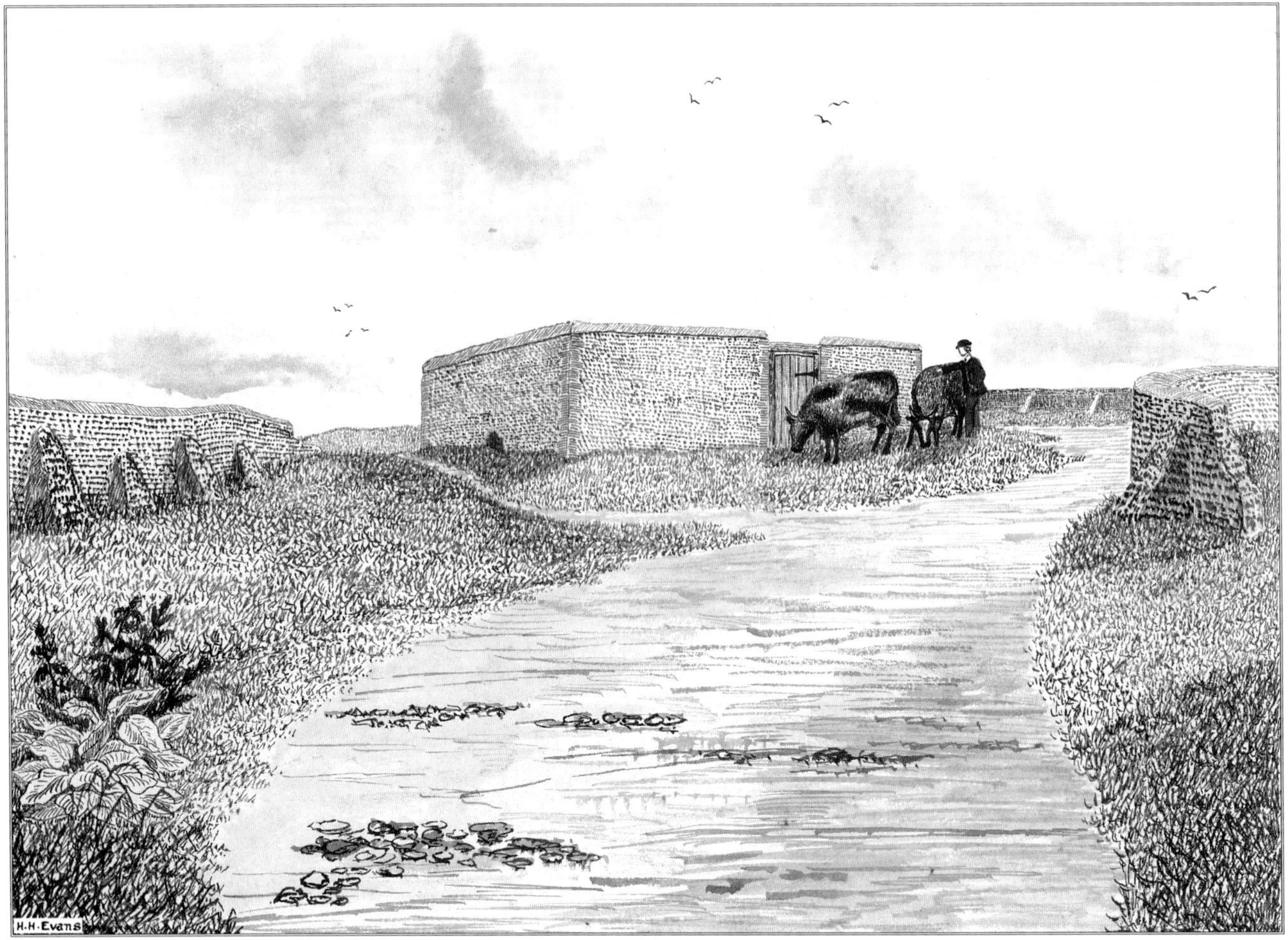

—— OLD POUND GREEN LANES, – LOOKING NORTH. ——

The Pound was used to keep stray animals until claimed by their owners on payment of a fine.
The Pound was situated to the sea side of Green Lanes. (Size of original drawing 155 x 210mm)

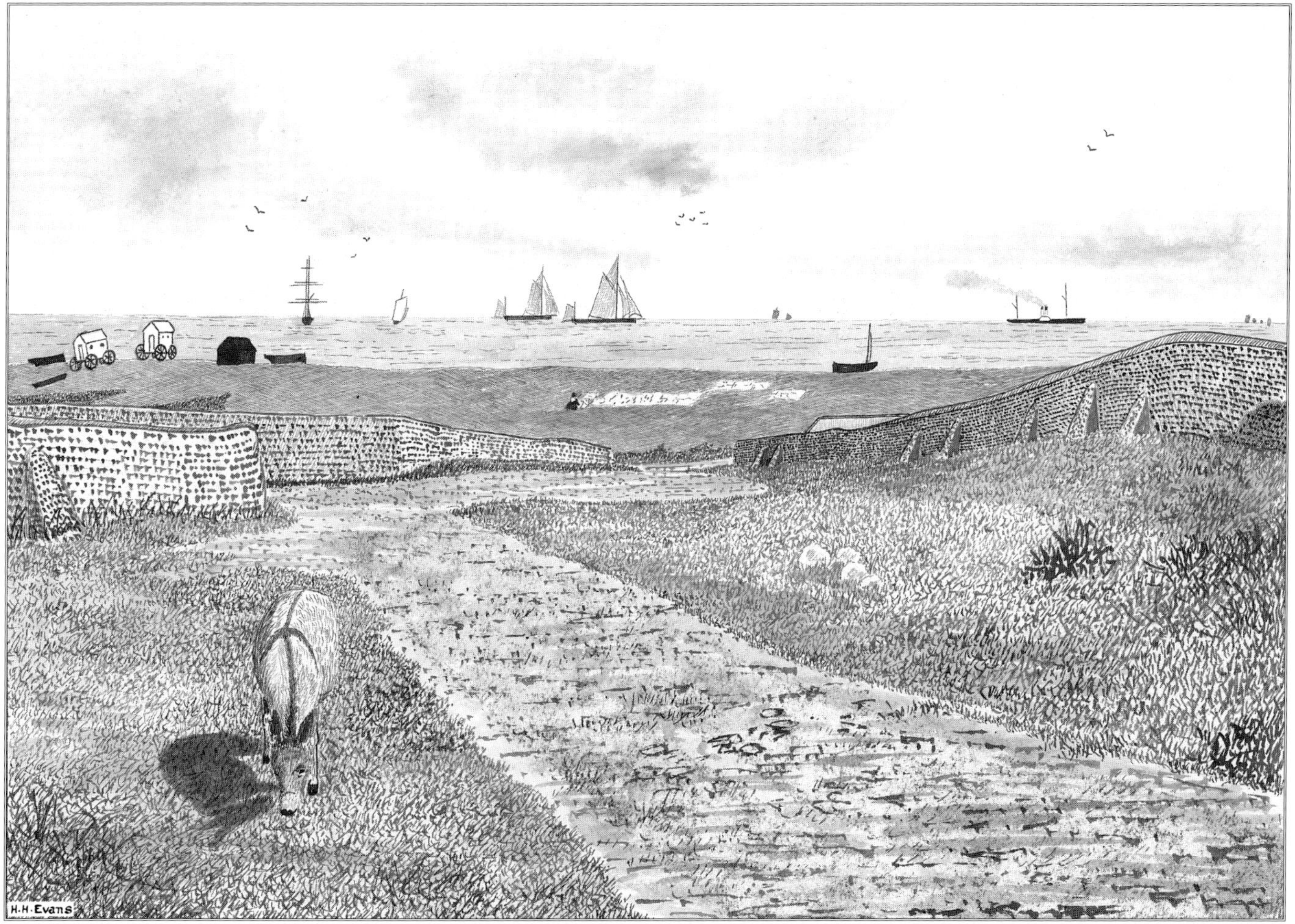

THE SEA FROM THE OLD POUND.

The beach from The Pound. Note the washing bleaching on the beach and the paddle steamer heading for Newhaven.
(Size of original drawing 155 x 210mm)

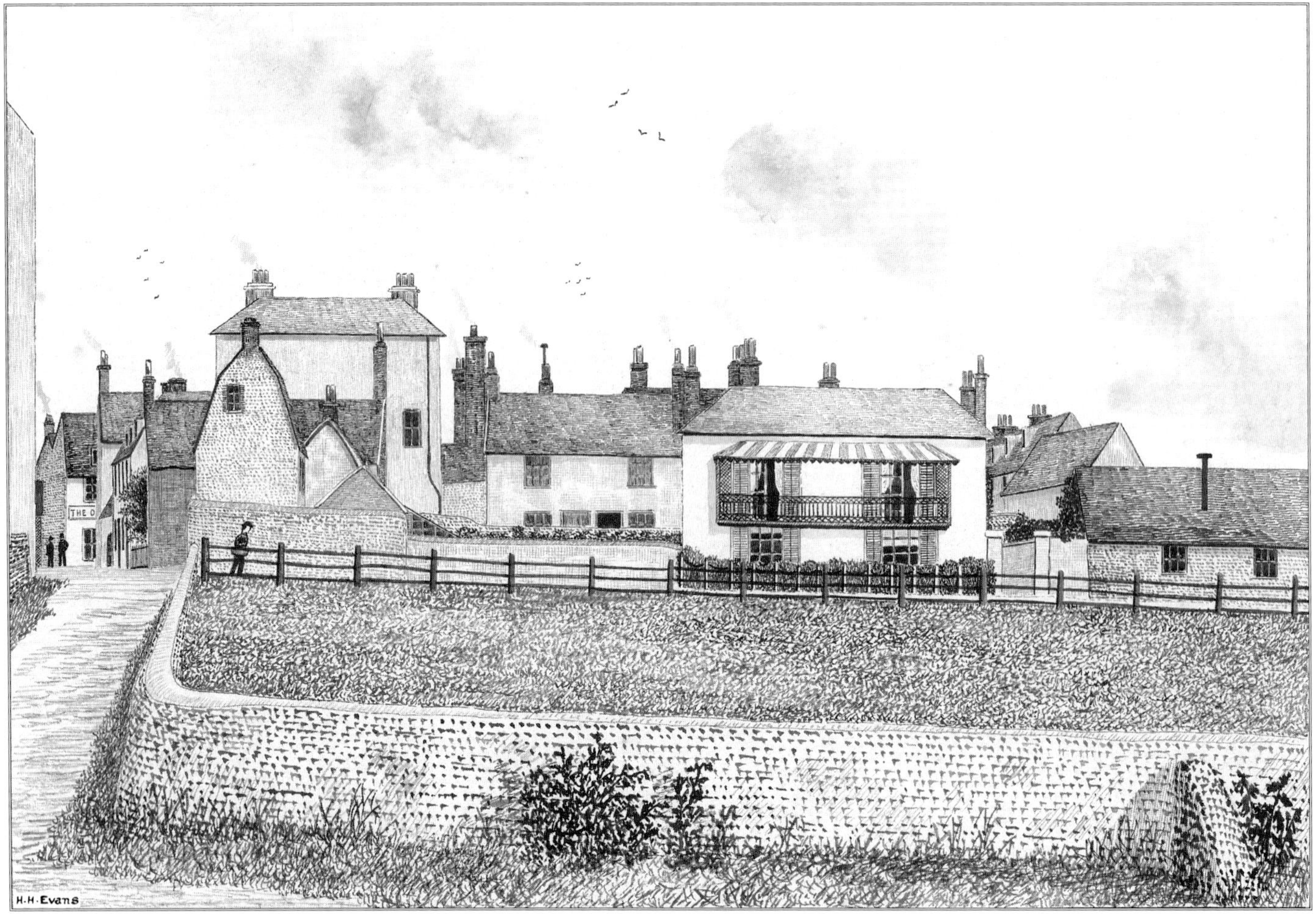

—— BAY HOUSE, ANGEL COTTAGES & WEST LANE. ——

—— BAY HOTEL AND GOLF HQ QUARTERS NOW STAND ON SITE ——

Pulled down in 1868.

The intersection of West Street and Pelham Place. The house on the right of the picture still exists. (Size of original drawing 160 x 210mm)

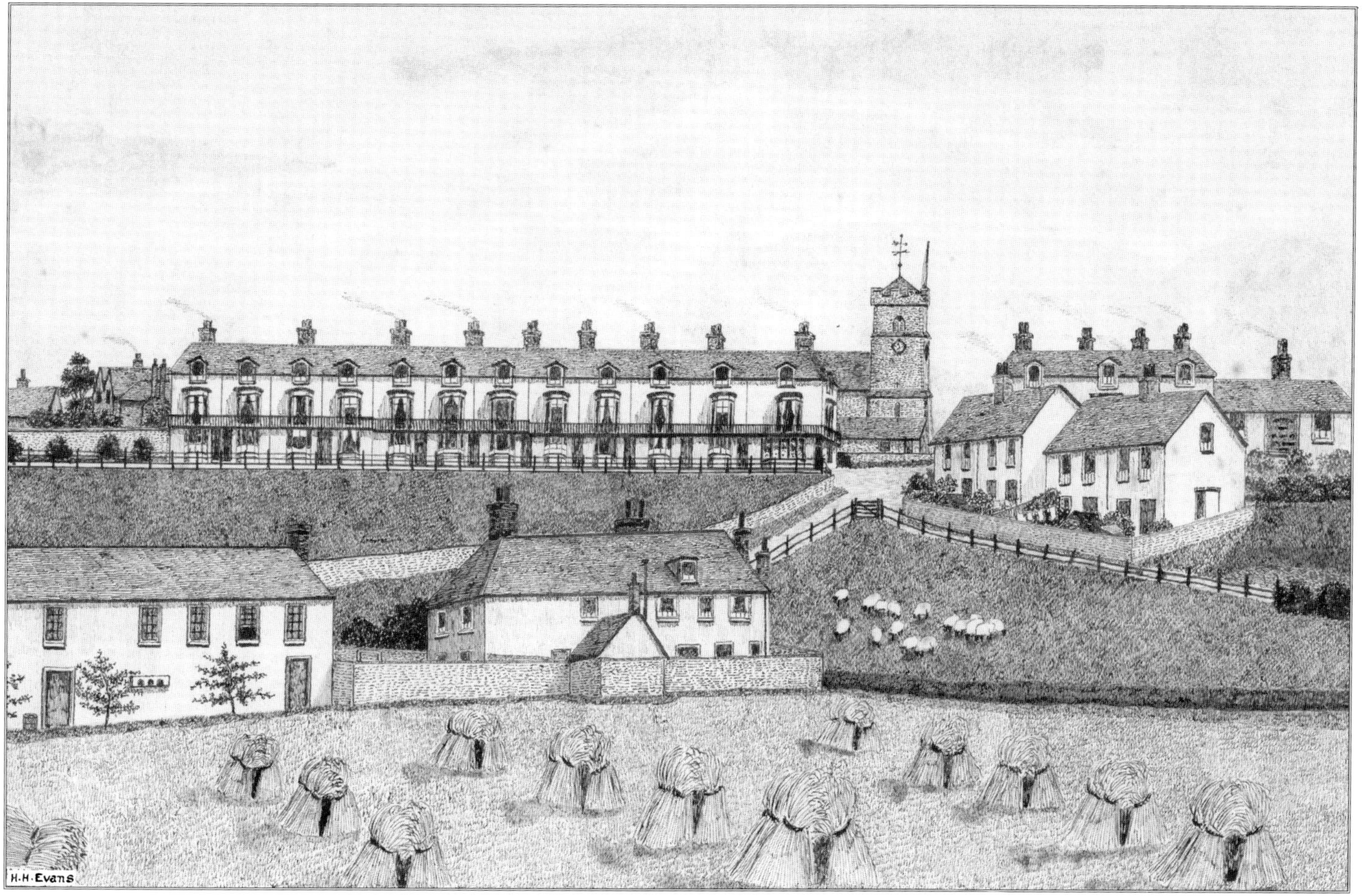

CLINTON PLACE, *FROM THE CORNFIELDS,* CLAREMONT ROAD, 1870.

Clinton Place was then all private houses, except No. 1 Woolgar's, the Ironmongers.

Clinton Place when houses had been built only on the south side. In the foreground of the drawing is Twynne House and the Dann Brook ran along the side of the cornfield. (Size of original drawing 285 x 180mm)

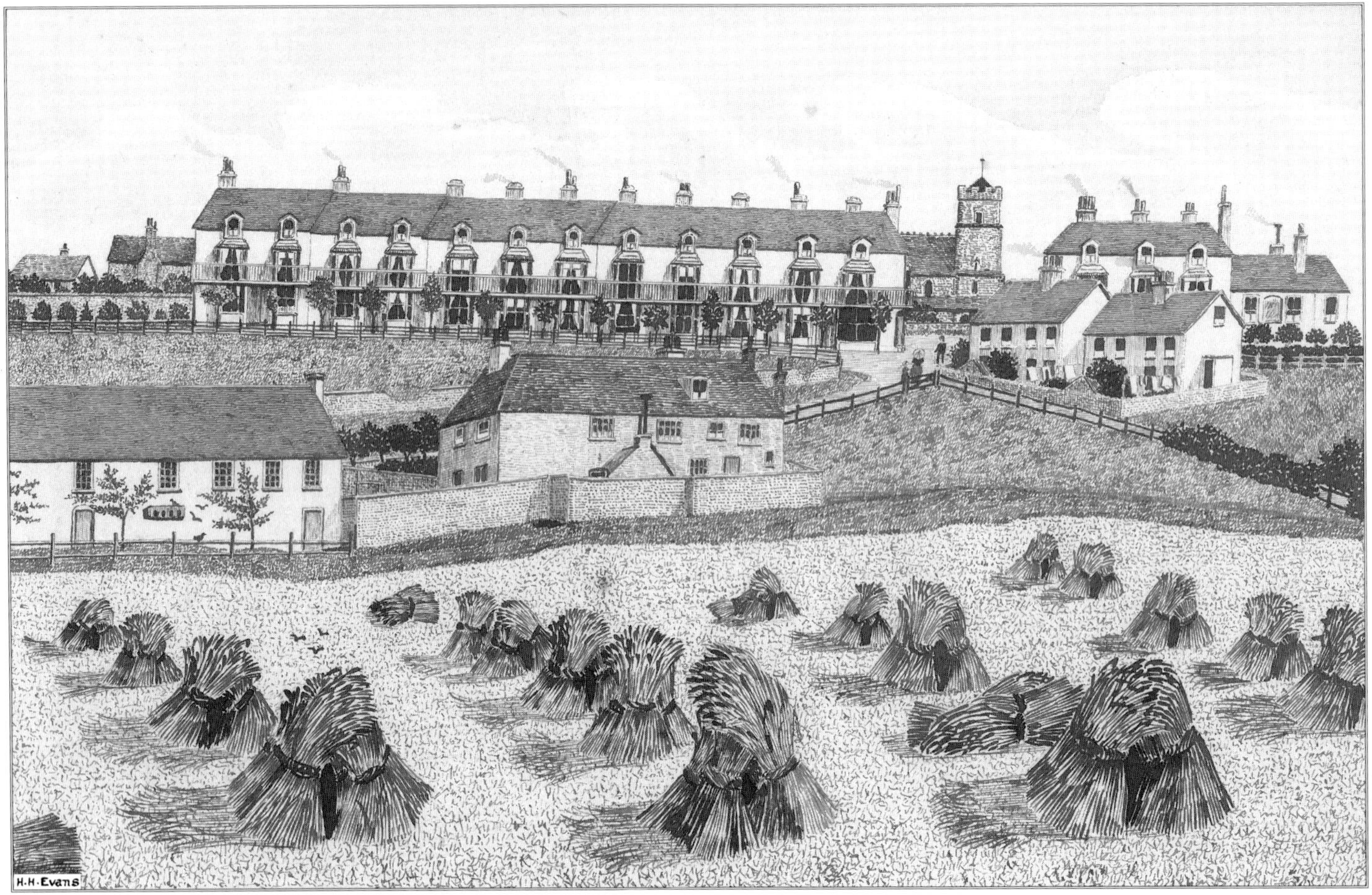

CLINTON PLACE, SEAFORD, FROM THE CORNFIELDS, BLATCHINGTON,
1870

A second view of Clinton Place. Note that trees have appeared in this drawing. Evans lived with his aunt for a time at number 6 and it can be seen that this drawing is centred on his house. (Size of original drawing 190 x 299mm)

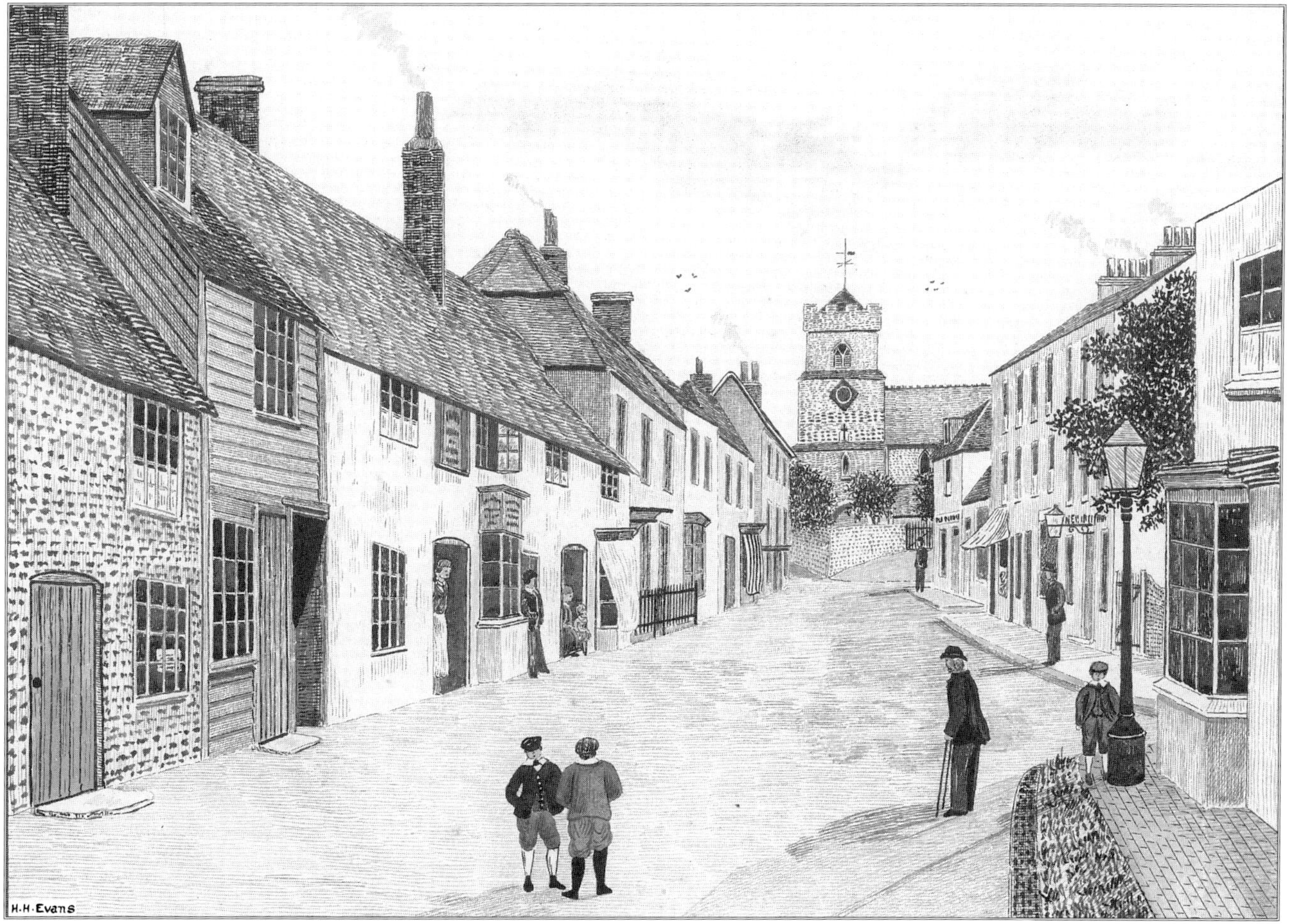

Church Street in 1875. Note that the lych gate for the church had yet to be built (1896).
The cottages on the left were destroyed by enemy action during World War Two. (Size of original drawing 160 x 210mm)

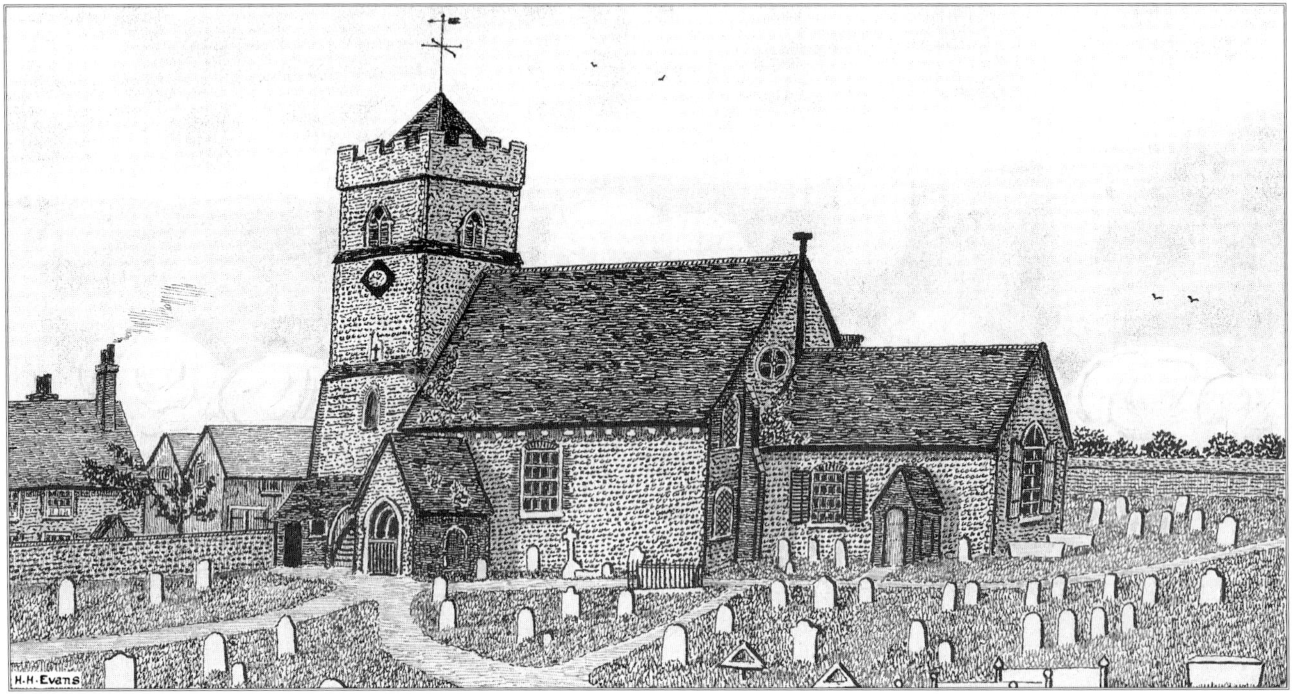

The church consists of a tower, nave, north and south aisles, and a kind of "apartment at the east end resembling an inn parlour, with sash windows and shutters complete.
Mark Antony Lower. M.A., F.S.A.

The register is one of the oldest in this part of England dating back to 1558, and is entitled "A Register Booke in parchment, for the Towne of Seaforde."

St. Leonard's Church, Seaford, before the restoration of 1862. Pear Tree Cottage and Wood's slaughterhouse that are shown on page 35 can be seen to the left of the drawing. (Size of original drawing 175 x180mm)

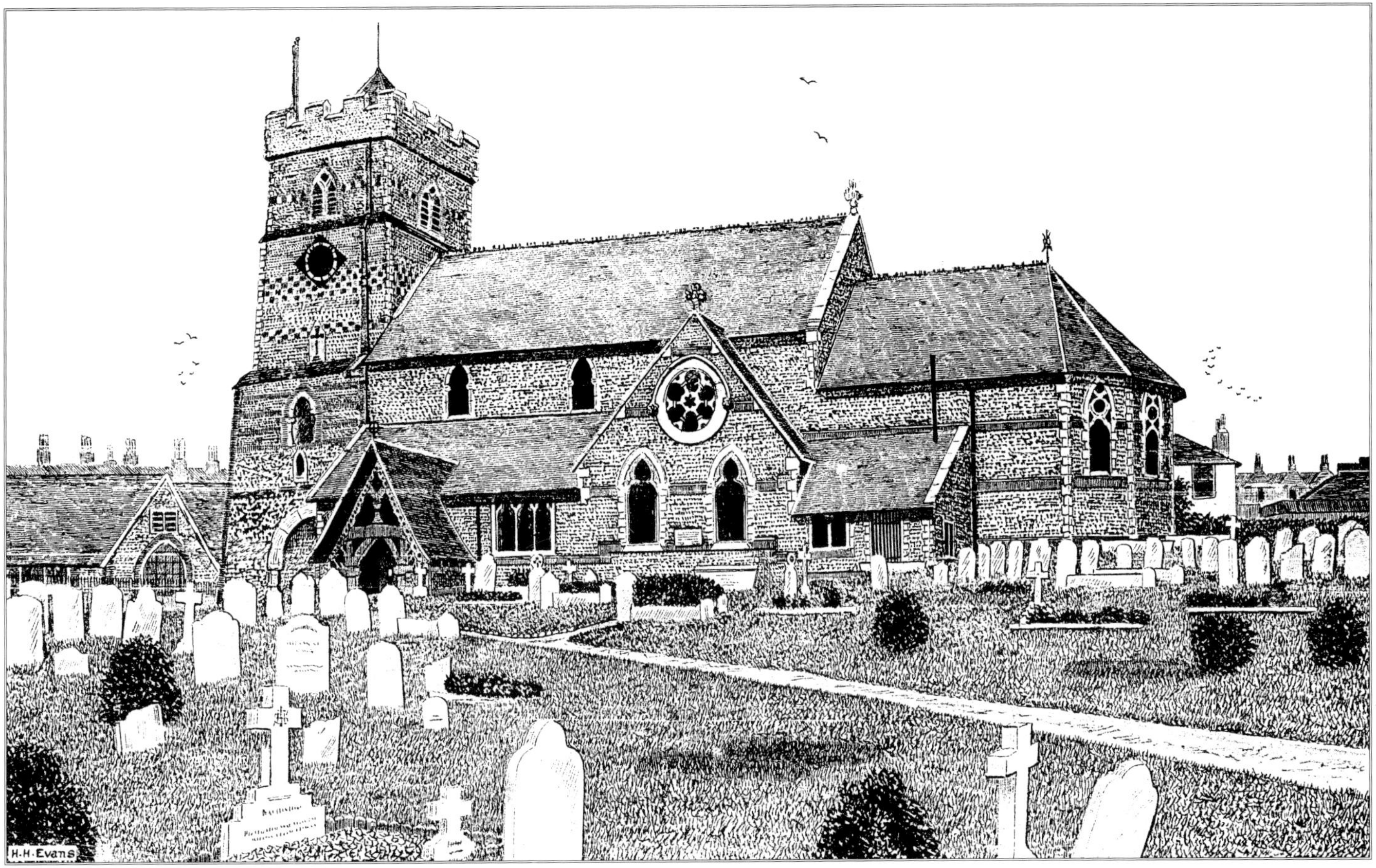

Seaford Church 1904.

St. Leonard's Church after restoration.
(Size of original drawing 190 x 280mm)

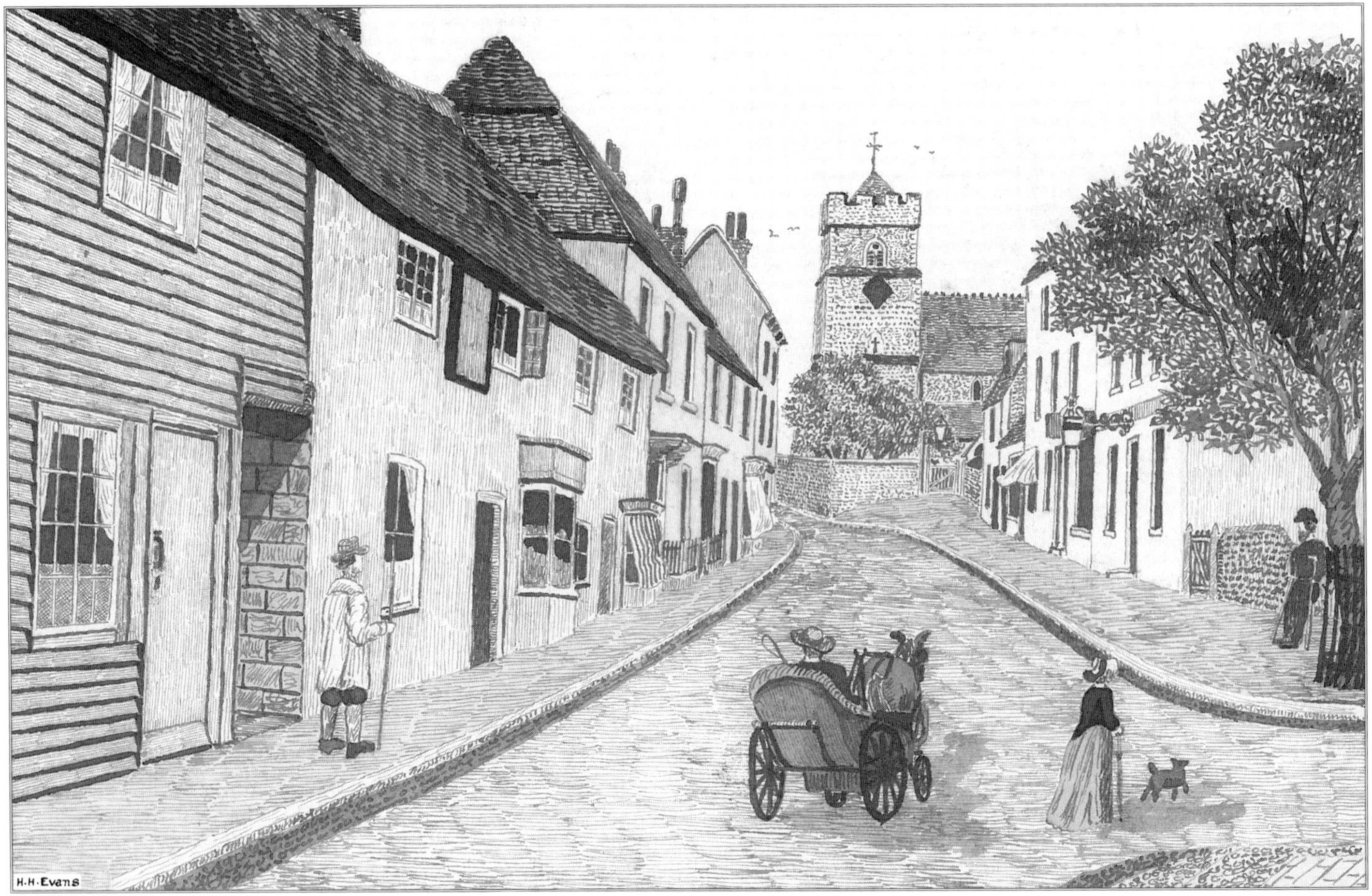

CHURCH ST, SEAFORD 1880.

Church Street in 1880.
(Size of original drawing 160 x 210mm)

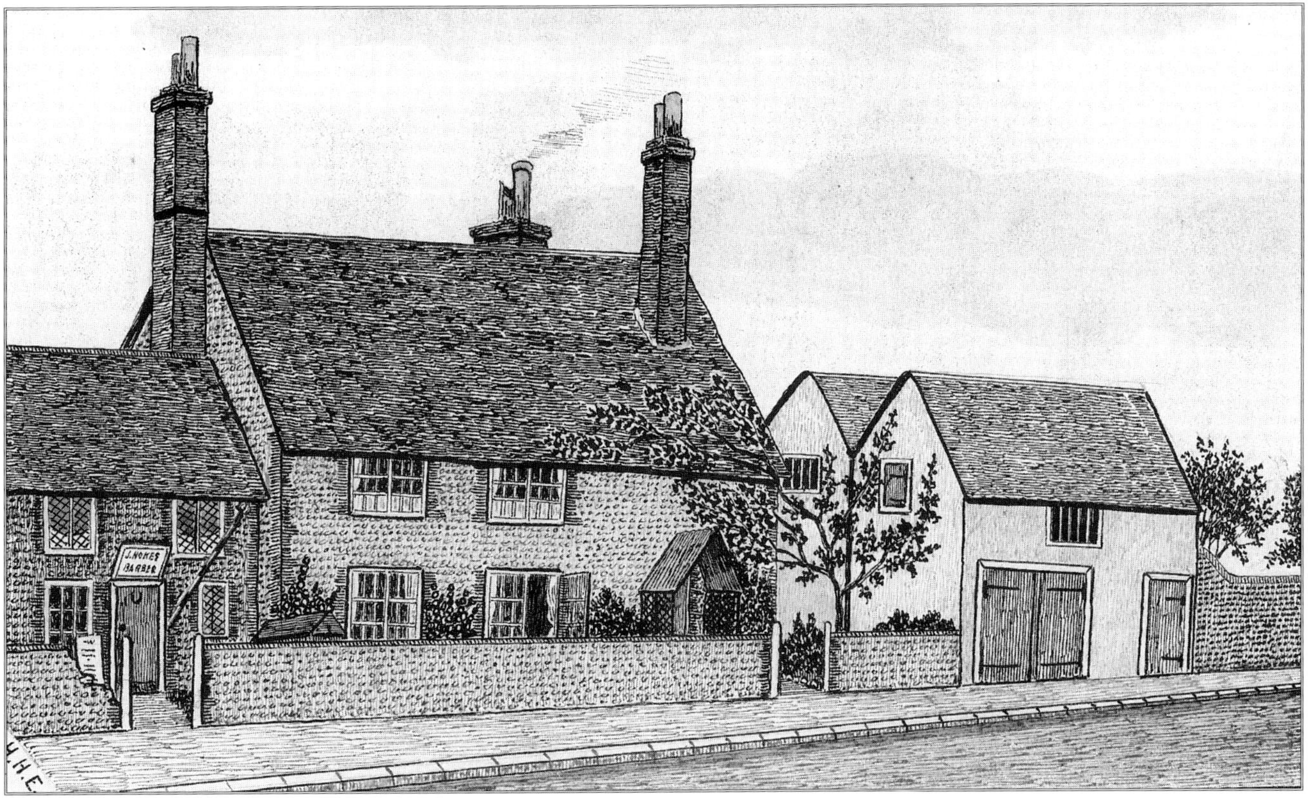

PEAR TREE COTTAGE AND WOOD'S SLAUGHTER HOUSE

OPPOSITE THE CHURCH IN CHURCH STREET.

Two shops now occupy the site of the cottages. Part of the girls school and play ground where the slaughter house stands.

Pear Tree Cottage and Wood's Slaughterhouse in Church Street. They stood approximately on the site of the present Post Office.

(Size of original drawing 160 x180mm)

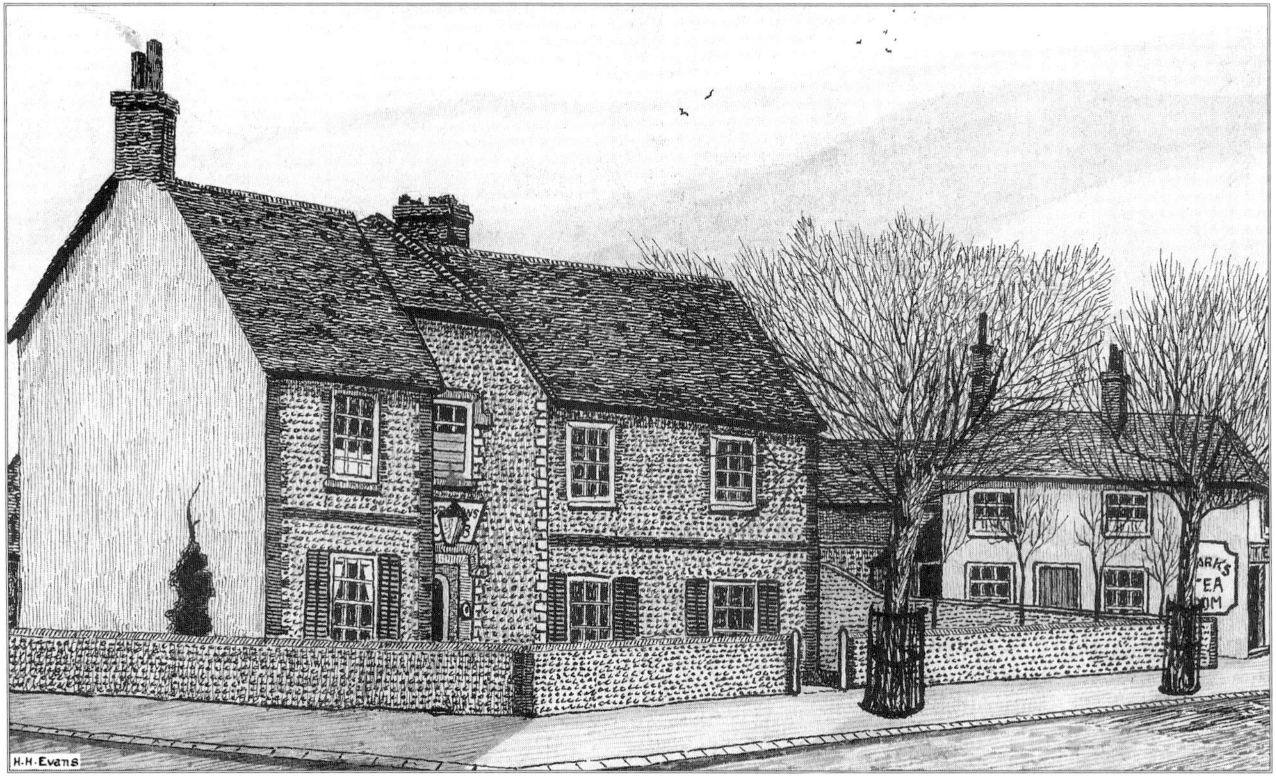

OLD WORKMANS CLUB & CLARKS-BAKEHOUSE,
CHURCH STREET.

This building was pulled down being unsafe in 1897, and three shops built. During the opperation the two fine horse-chesnuts trees were so damaged that they soon after died.

The old Workman's Club is difficult to place as the drawings vary greatly and the corner appears as a curve. It is possible that this is the corner of Church Lane. (Size of original drawing 170 x 180mm)

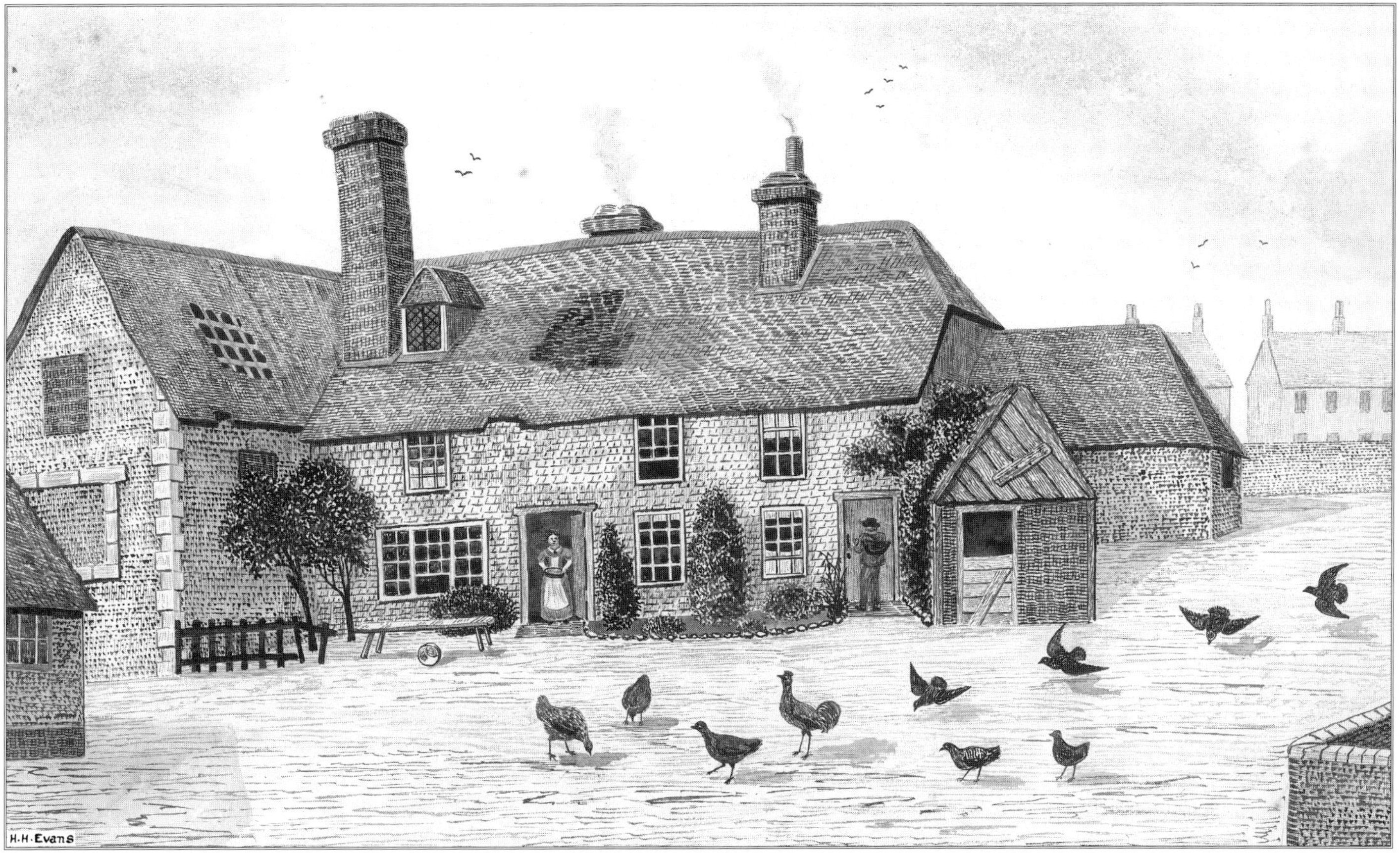

COTTAGES BACK OF WORKMAN'S CLUB.
— PULLED DOWN IN 1897 — AND STABLES BUILT. —

Cottages at the rear of the Workman's Club are again difficult to place but may have been replaced by the stables in Phoenix Court.
The drawing is dated 1904.
(Size of original drawing 185 x 295mm)

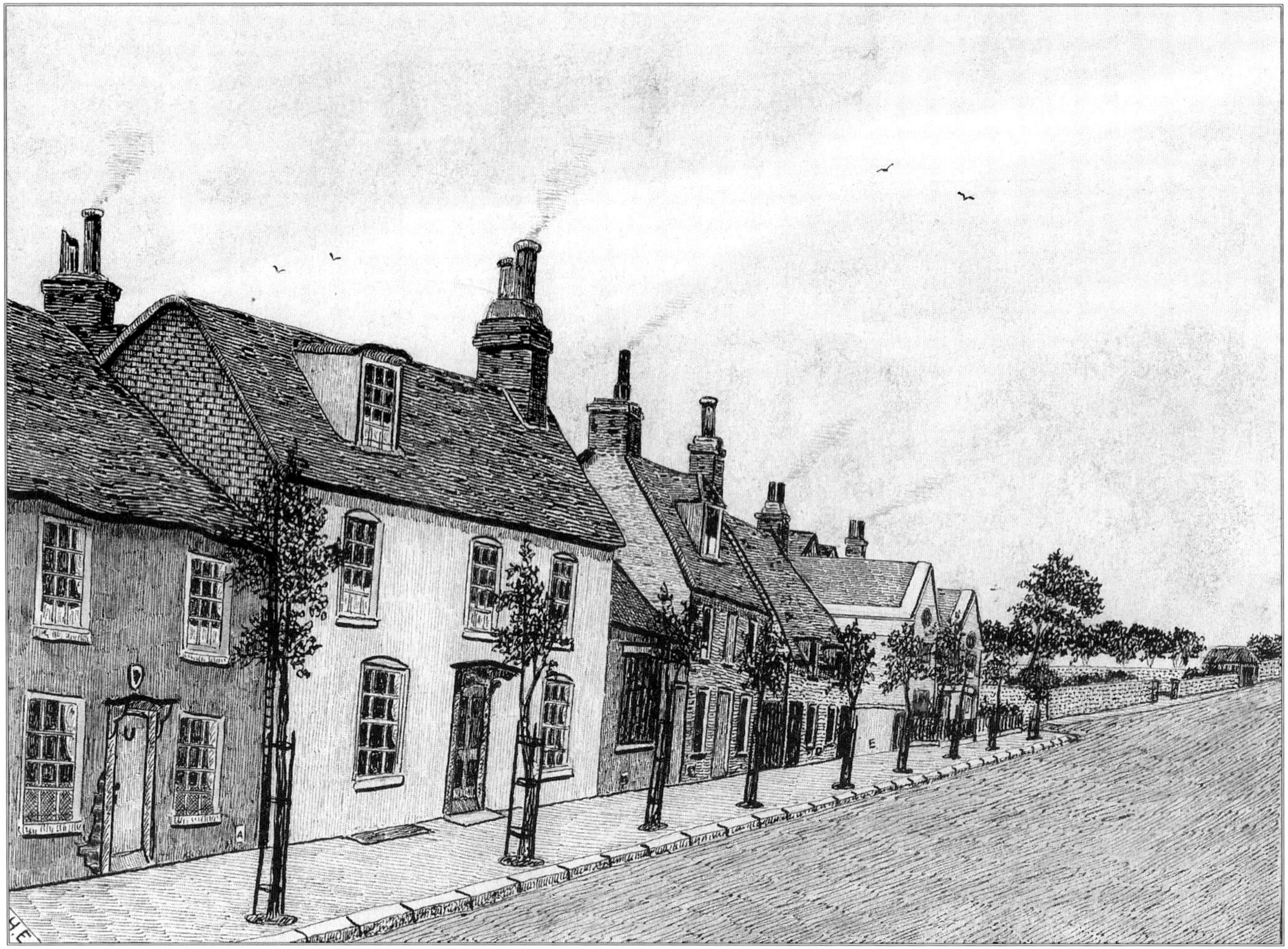

The west side of Broad Street. The corner of Place Lane can be seen to the right of centre.
(Size of original drawing 170 x180mm)

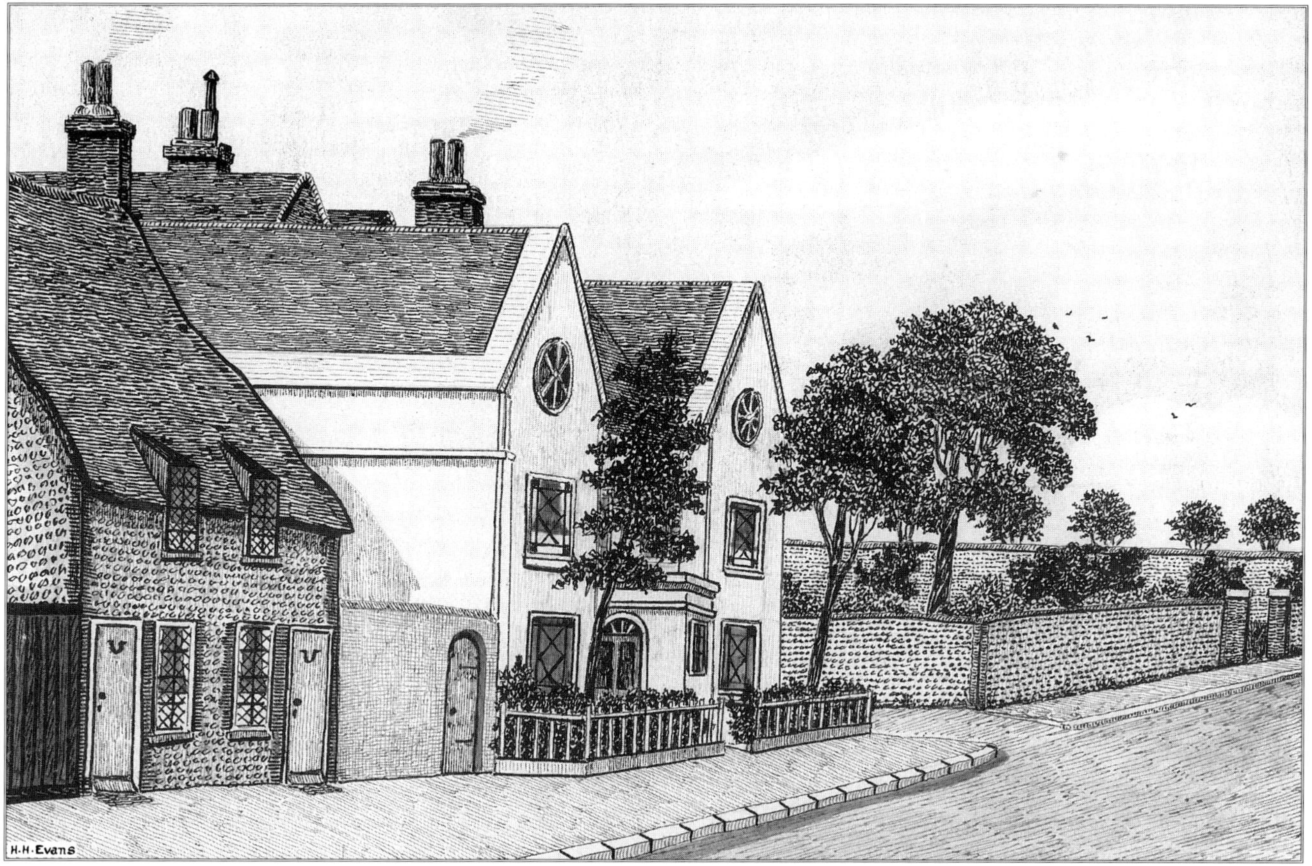

GABLE END, BROAD ST 1902.

Is now two shops and the Post Office built where the two cottages stand. These cottages were the only one's in Seaford with Sussex Dormer windows.

Detailed view of Gable End, a house that stood on the corner of Place Lane and Broad Street. (Size of original drawing 160 x 180mm)

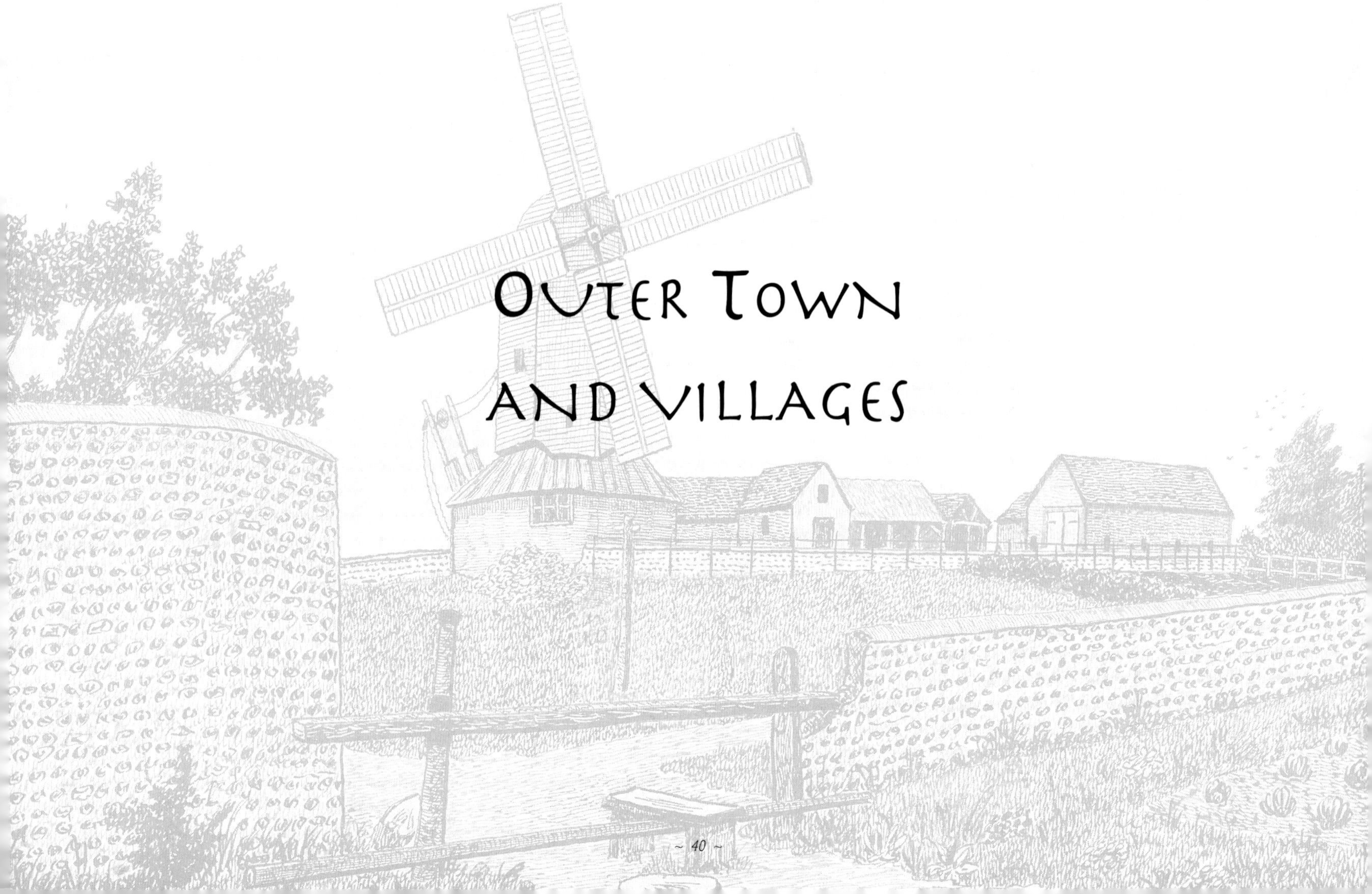

Outer Town and Villages

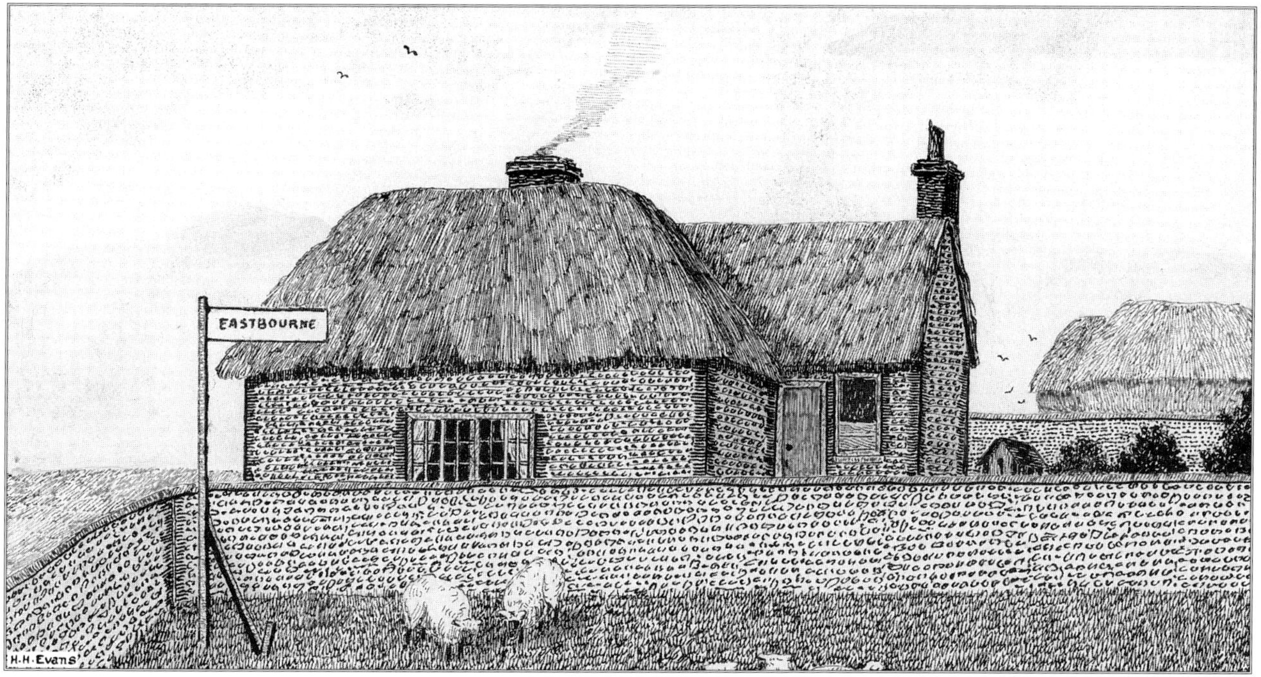

OLD THATCHED COTTAGE, CORNER OF SUTTON ROAD, FACING BROAD STREET.

The field in foreground extended from Broad St. to East Street & from Sutton Road to Croft Lane. In this field at the corner of East St. and Croft Lane stood an old Elm tree – hence "Elm Brewery."

Bravery's shop now stands where the cottage is seen, and Barbers' &c. in the field where the signpost is, which was tall so that it could be seen coming up Broad St. and also from Clinton Place.

Sutton Road was not so wide then, and from Pigeon House farm to Sutton Mill the foot path was on the top of the bank, on the left hand side going to the Mill.

This drawing shows the junction of Broad Street and Sutton Road, which was the main road from the town - signposted to Eastbourne.
(Size of original drawing 185 x 180mm)

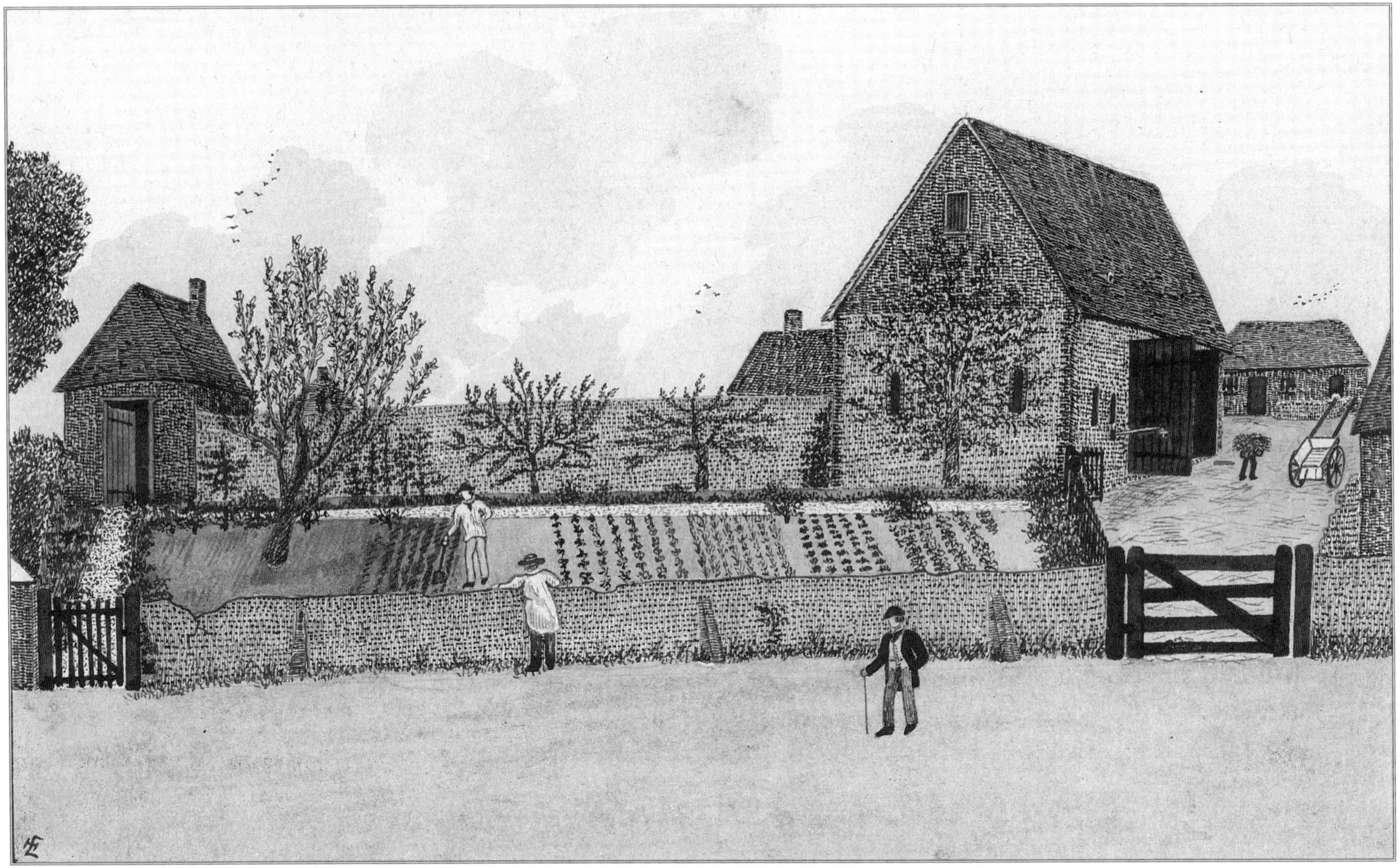

PIGEON-HOUSE FARM, Sutton Road, NOW BUILT OVER.

Pigeon House Farm lay on the north-west side of Sutton Road.
(Size of original drawing 145 x 225mm)

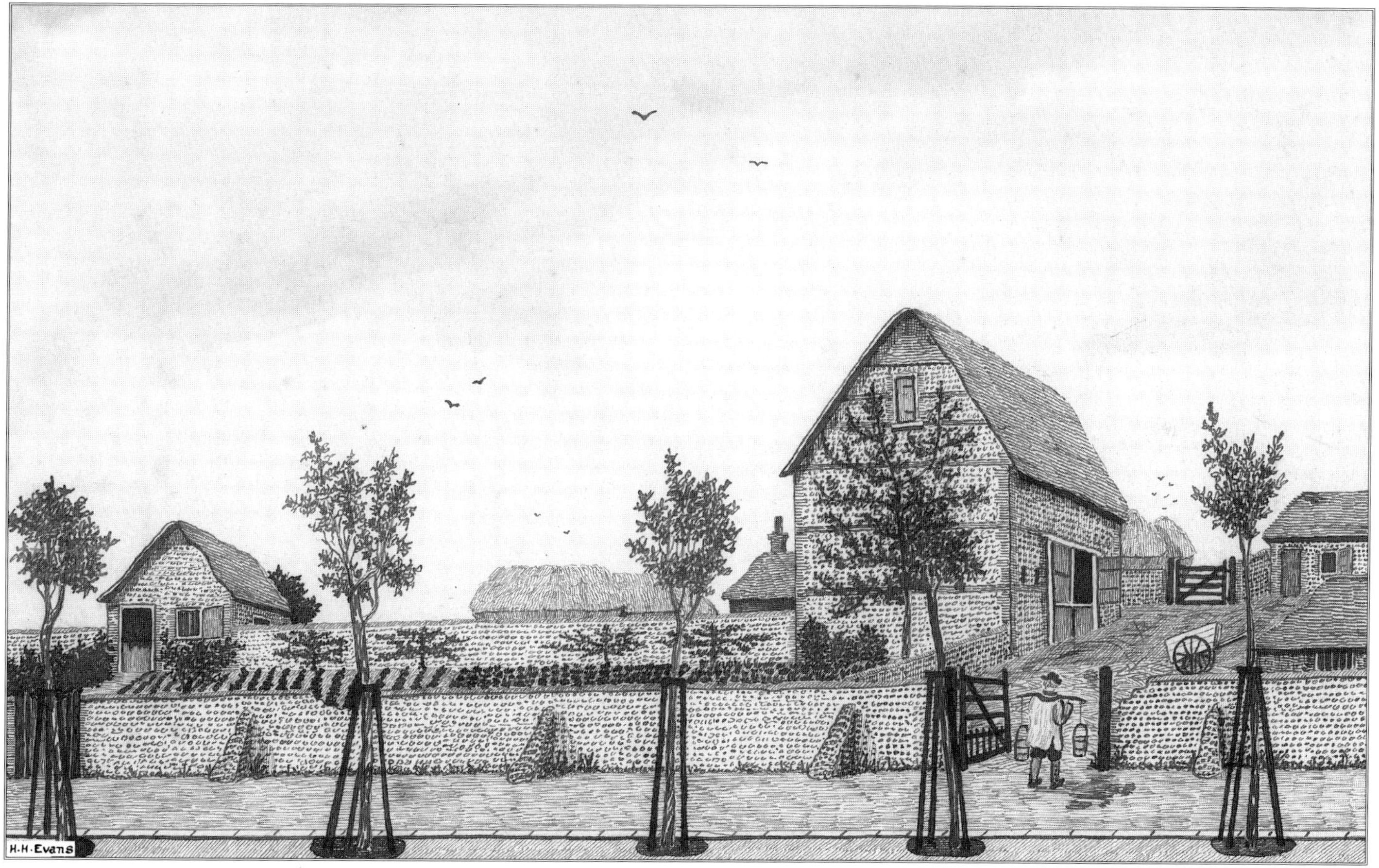

PIGEON-HOUSE BARN, SUTTON ROAD. *Pulled down 1884.*

It was in this barn that the Tea, Coffee, Wheat, Linseed, Cotton & Indigo, was stored waiting sale, that was saved from the S.S. Gannet, wrecked, on the 14th February 1882.

Another view of Pigeon House Farm after the trees had been planted in Sutton Road. (Size of original drawing 160 x 230mm)

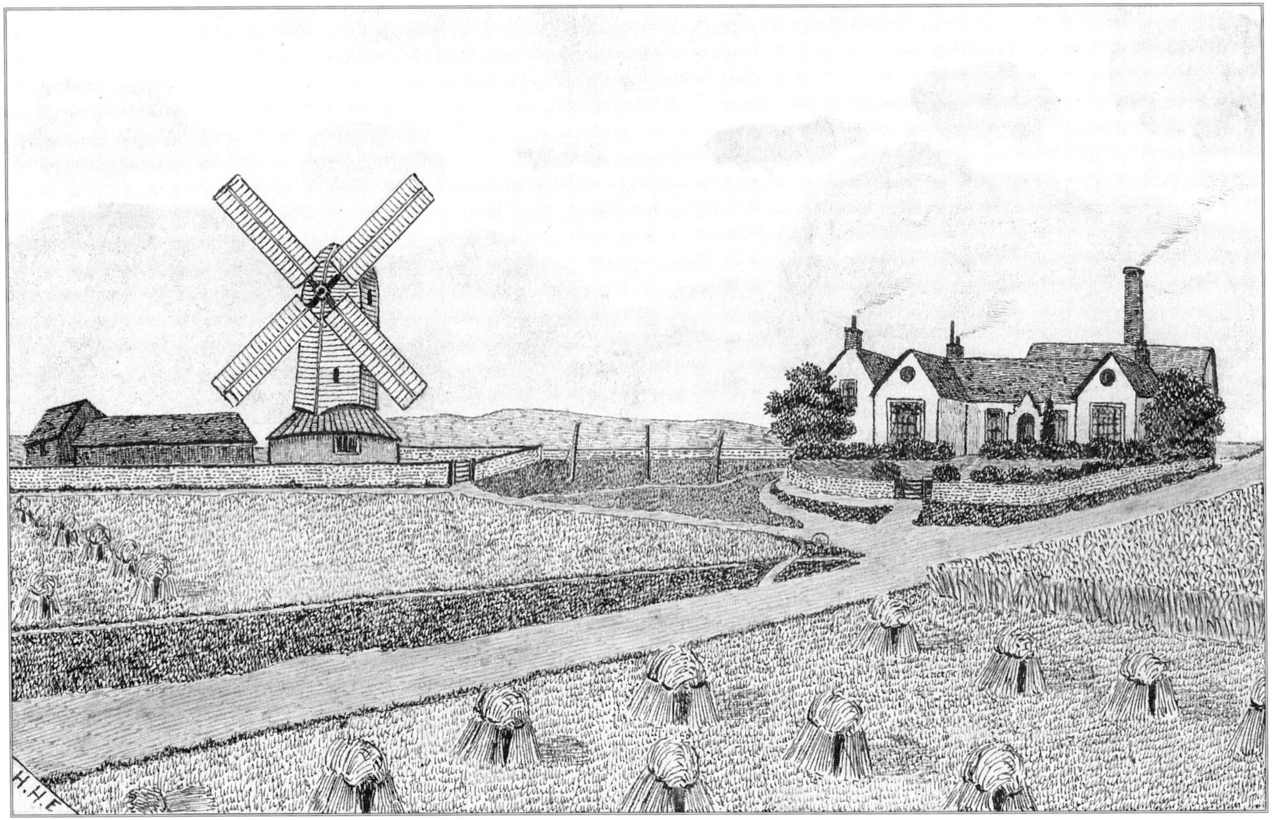

SUTTON MILL AND MILL HOUSE.

The Mill was worked and house inhabited by Thos. Ade for many years.
The Mill was dismantled in 1904, and
pulled down & houses built 1909.

Sutton Mill and Mill House. The Mill House is still in existence and Mill Drive and Milldown Road names point to the location of the Mill. (Size of original drawing 155 x 180mm)

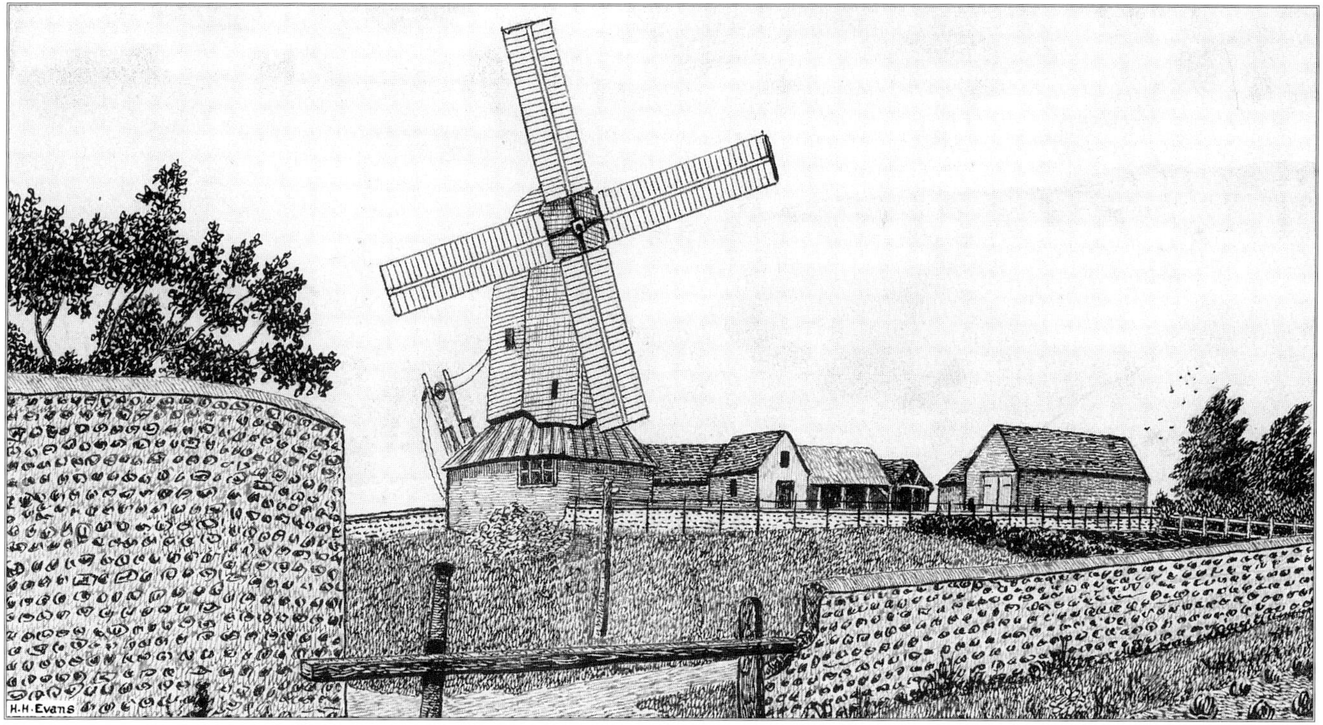

SUTTON MILL, *FROM THE FOOTPATH TO HINDOVER.*

Dismantled in **1904**.

Pulled down and houses built 1909.

There used to be a windmill at the back of the Queen's Hall facing the present Claremont Road, one near Seaford College (hence Millburgh) and the black wind-mill at Blatchington, near the house named Mill-house facing the farm-road to Bishopstone.

The post on the left hand side of style was part of the bowsprit of the Barque "Sagatun," wrecked at Seaford, 26th September 1900.

Another view of Sutton Mill showing a footpath to Hindover. There is still a footpath in this area. (Size of original drawing 185 x 180mm)

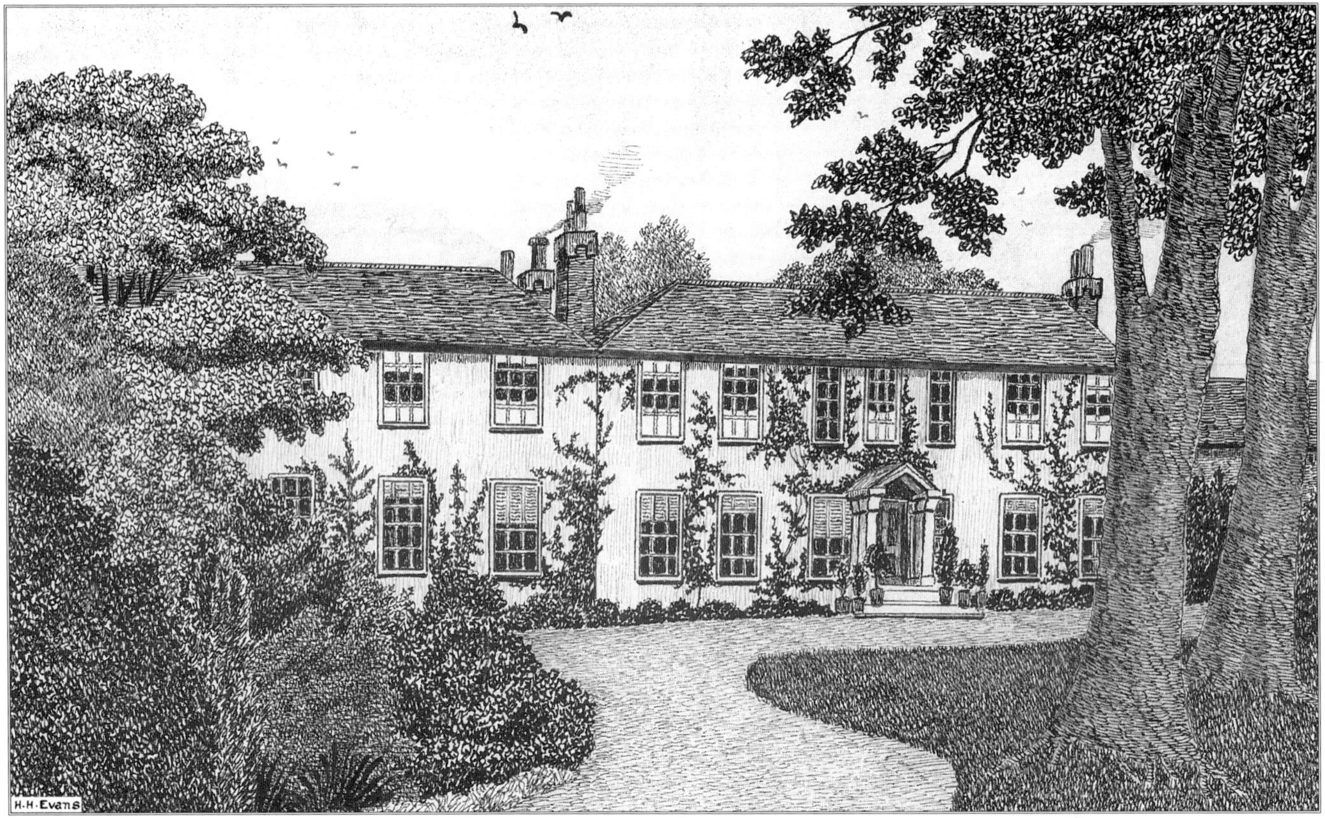

SUTTON PLACE 1910. { SEAFORD MANOR HOUSE. }

It was the property and residence of the Major Harisons for many years, it then passed into the hands, of Mr Hutchings, who bought the Sutton Estate. During the War 1914-18 The Canadians used it as a Kharki College. And now, after additions and alterations it is a boys school, and renamed Ashampstead.

Sutton Place in 1910. (Size of original drawing 170 x 180mm)

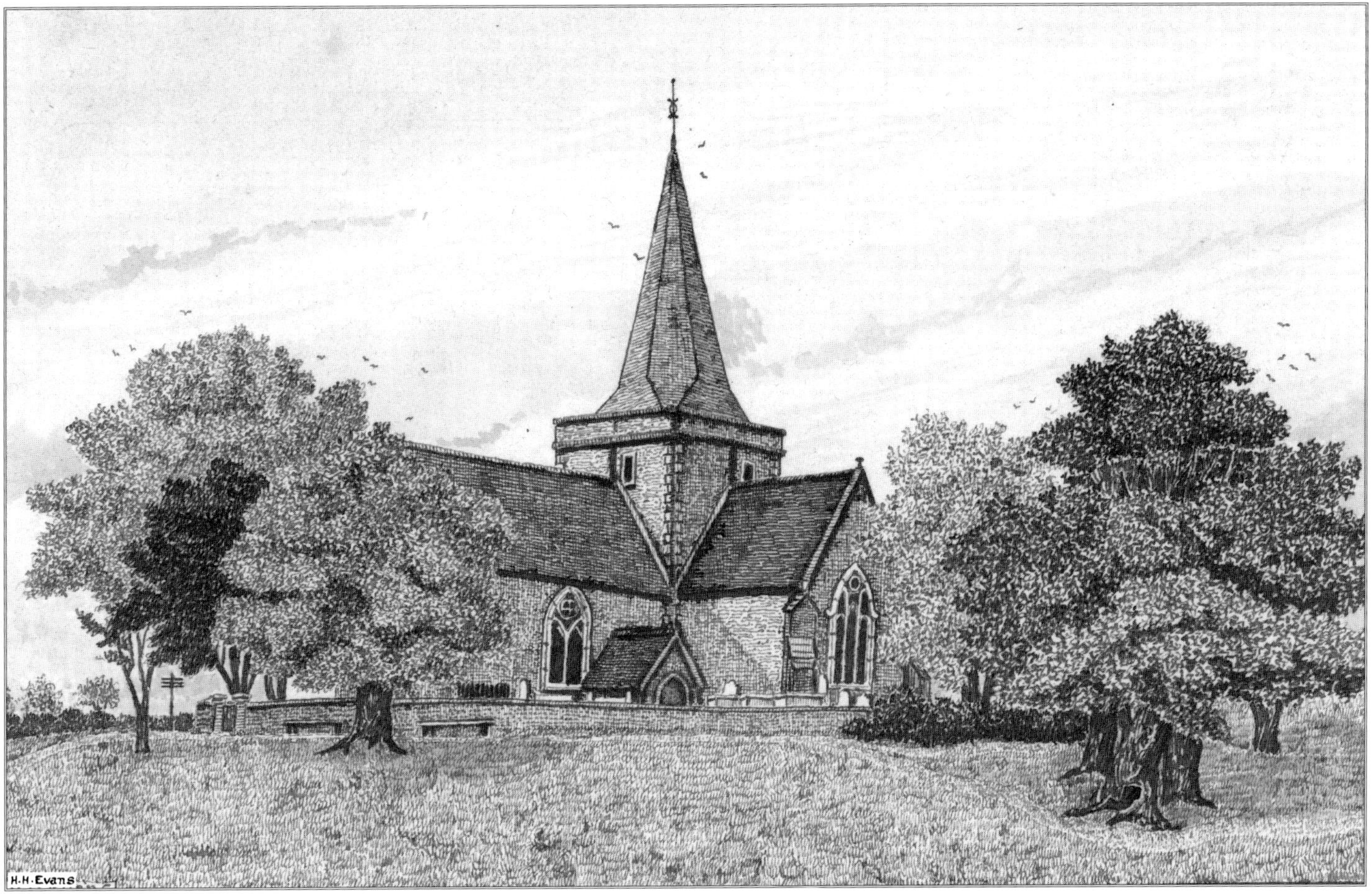

ALFRISTON CHURCH, DATE 1398.

The buttresses are of such massive proportions that the circumference of the Church is greater than the Churchyard which surrounds it.

Alfriston Church copied from a photograph by WR Wynter. (Size of original drawing 120 x 162mm)

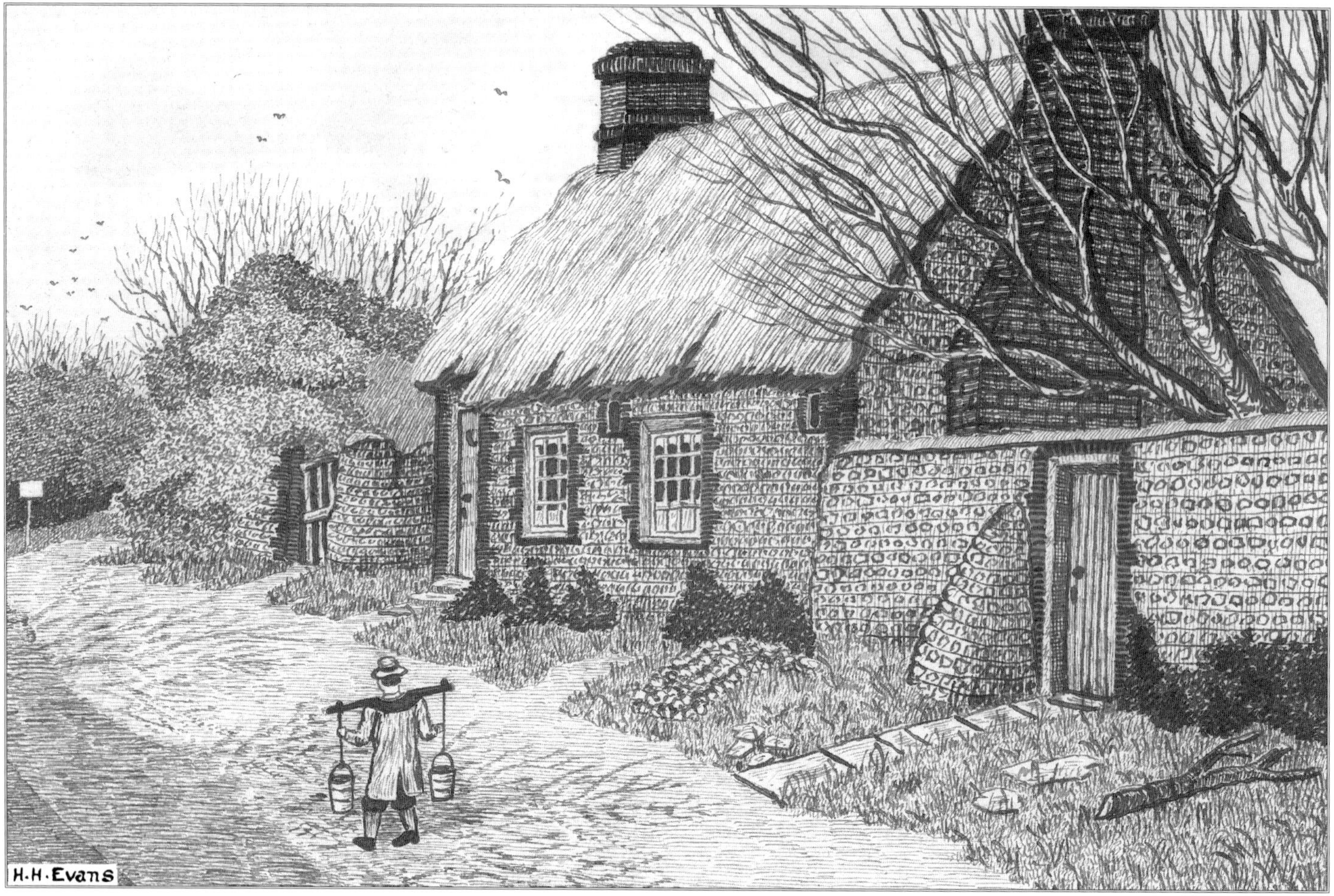

OLD COTTAGE, BLATCHINGTON.
Now the entrance to Arlington house

A cottage in Blatchington copied from a photograph by WR Wynter. (Size of original drawing 120 x 160mm)

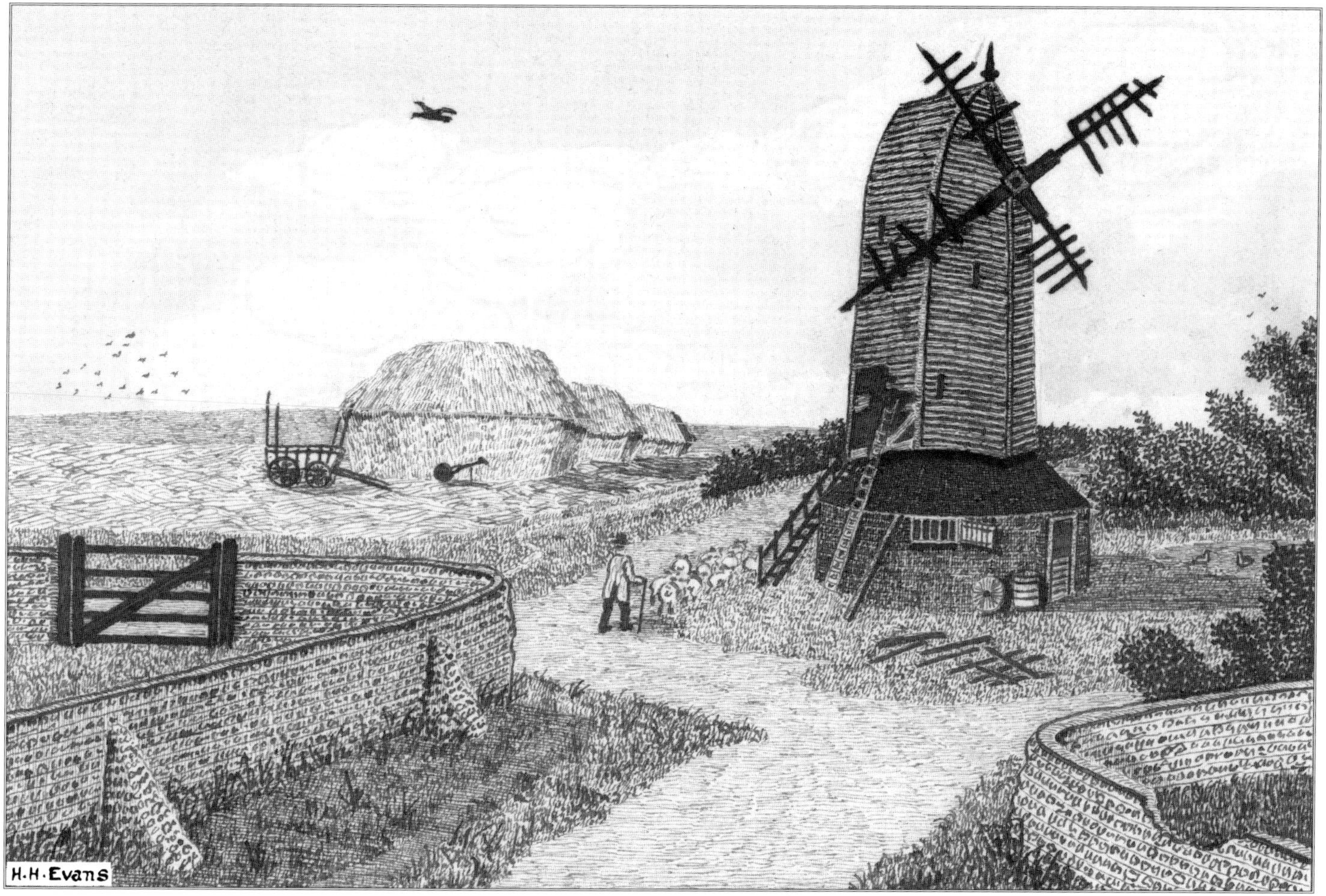

OLD BLACK WIND-MILL, BLATCHINGTON

The old windmill in Blatchington, known as the Black Windmill. Evans' source for the drawing is not known at present.
(Size of original drawing 115 x 160mm)

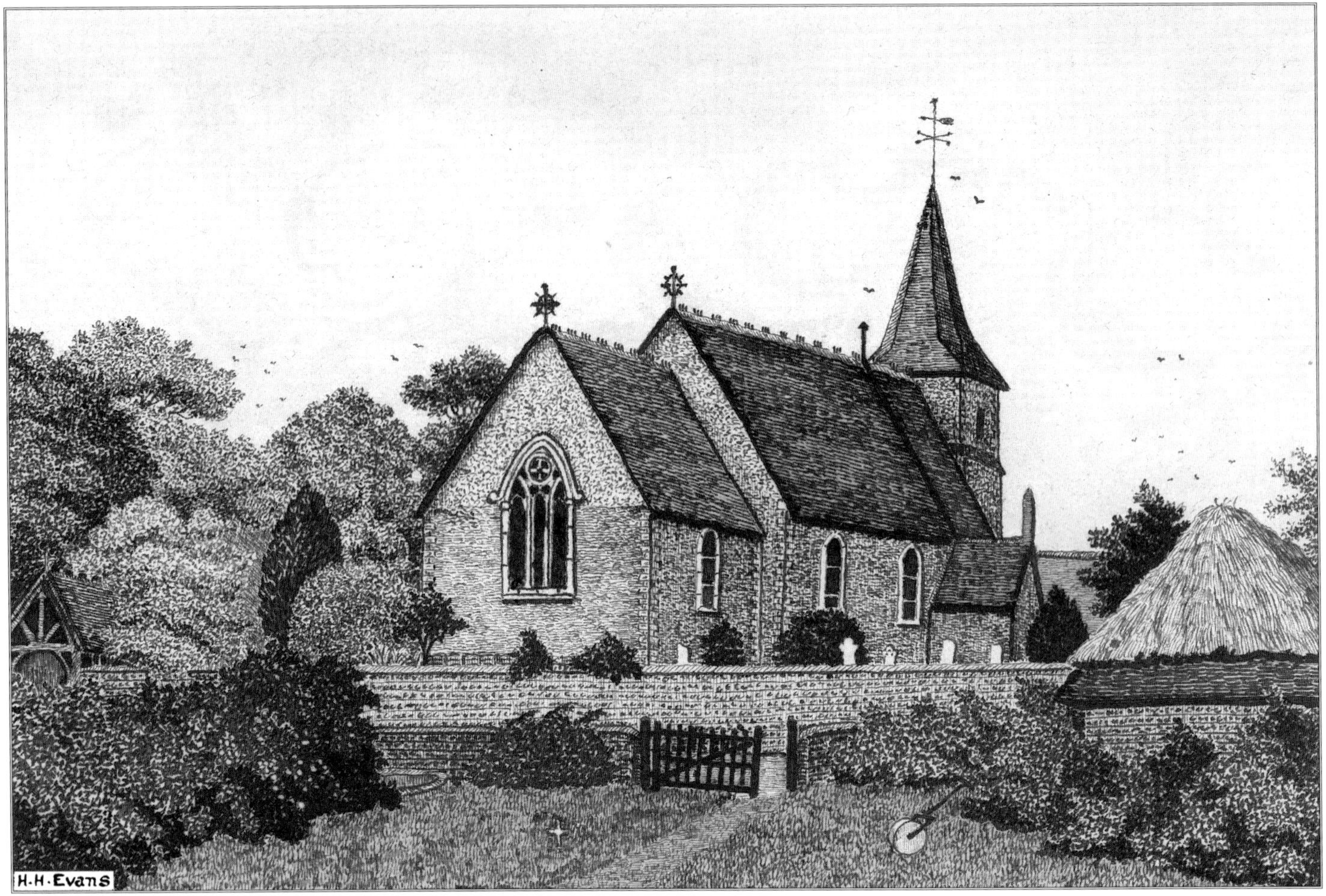

\+ BLATCHINGTON CHURCH

\+ A House now stands in this field.

Blatchington Church copied from a photograph by WR Wynter (Size of original drawing 115 x162mm)

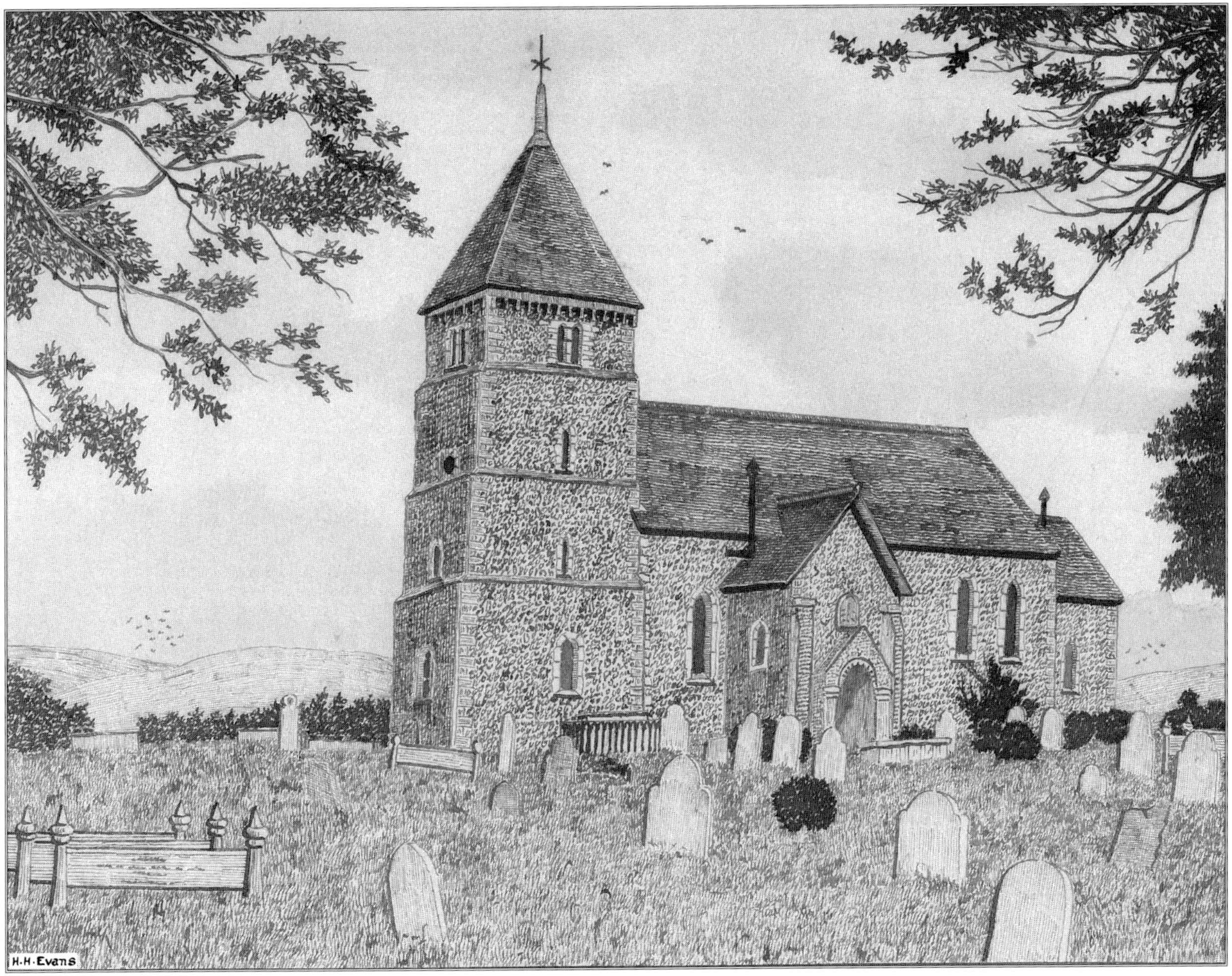

BISHOPSTONE CHURCH.

Bishopstone Church copied from a photograph by WR Wynter. (Size of original drawing 160 x 200mm)

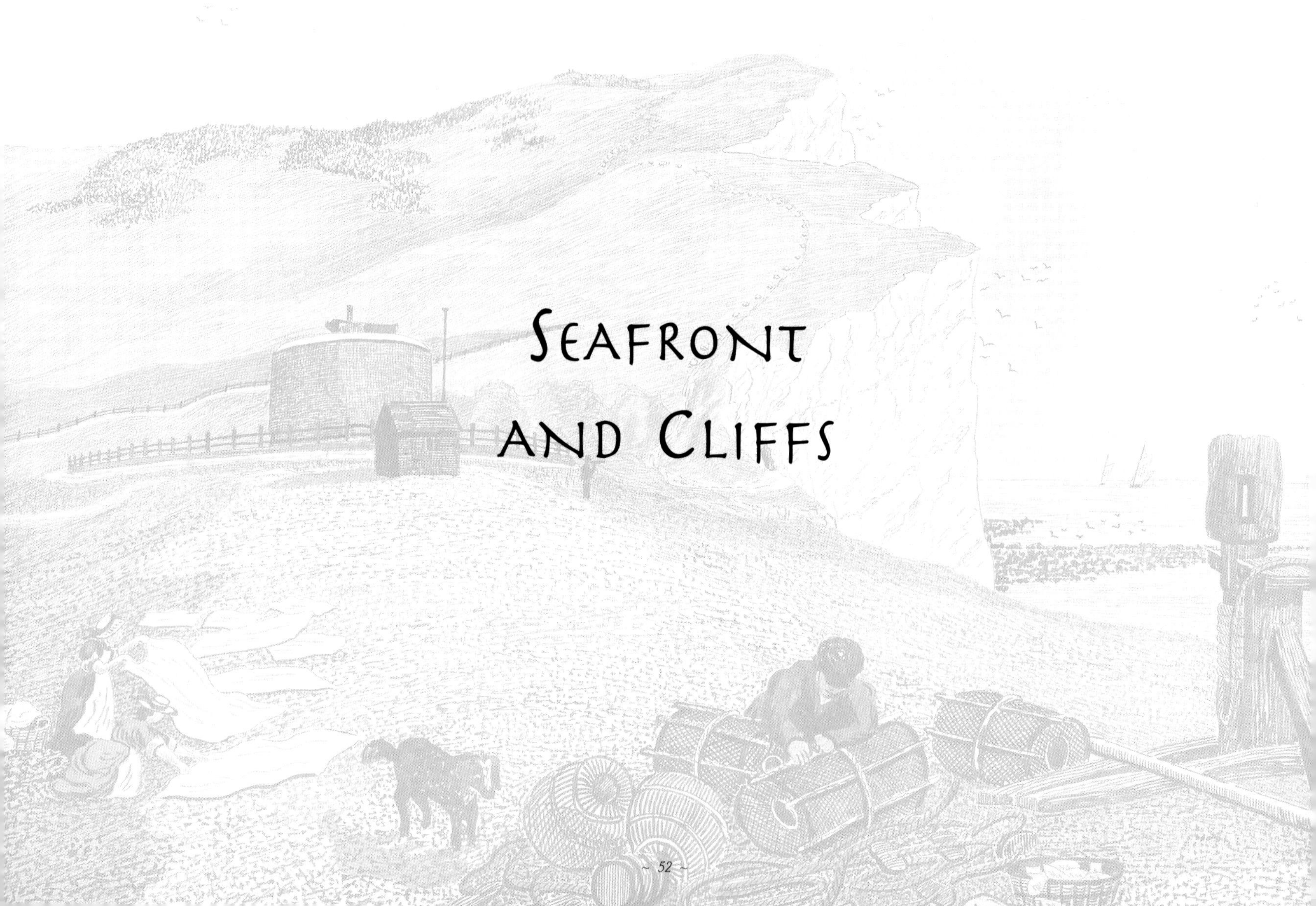

Seafront and Cliffs

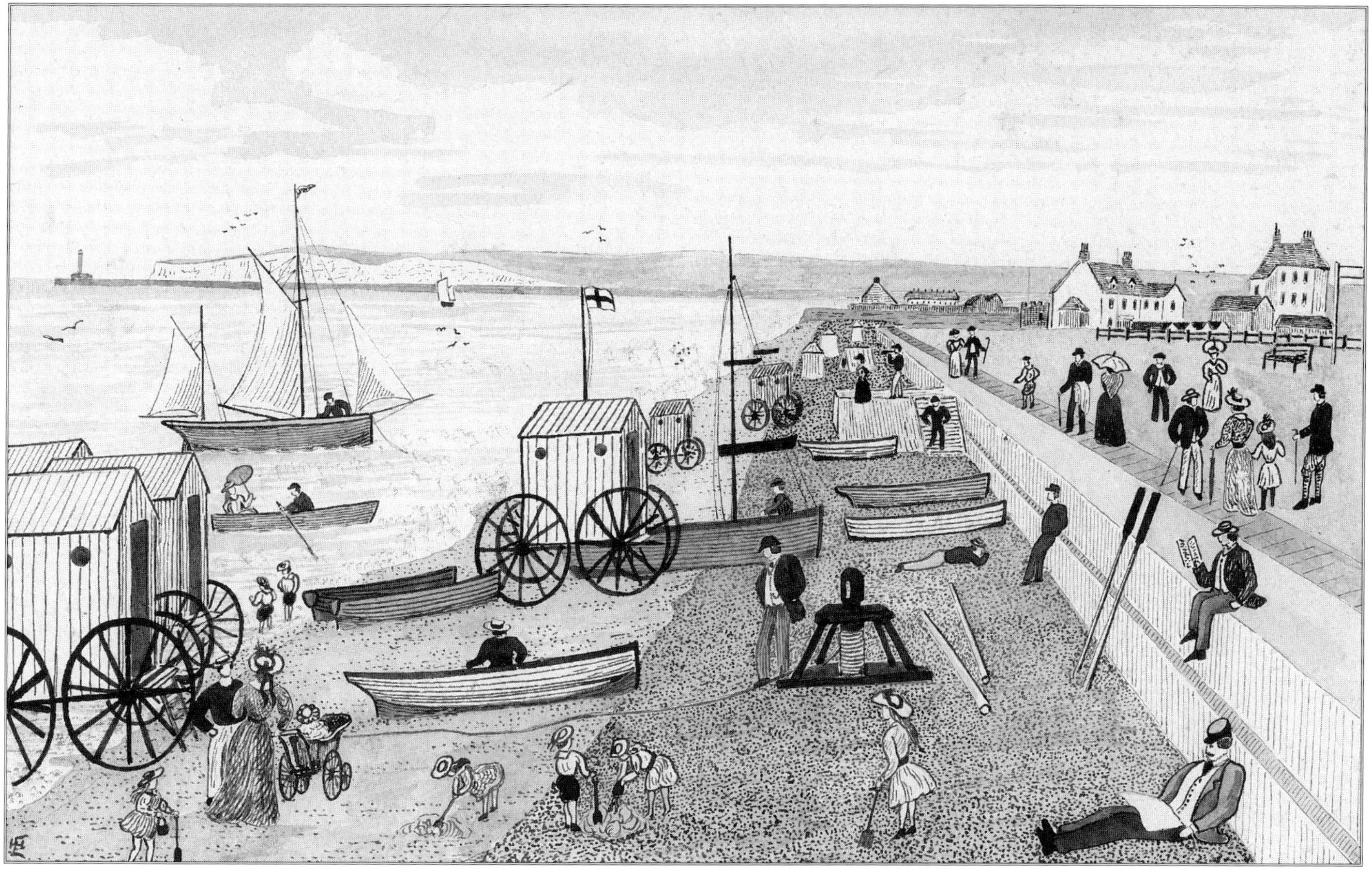

THE BEACH, — LOOKING WEST.

The beach looking west. Note the sea wall and steps down to the beach and the bathing machines that were winched in and out of the sea. (Size of original drawing 145 x 220mm)

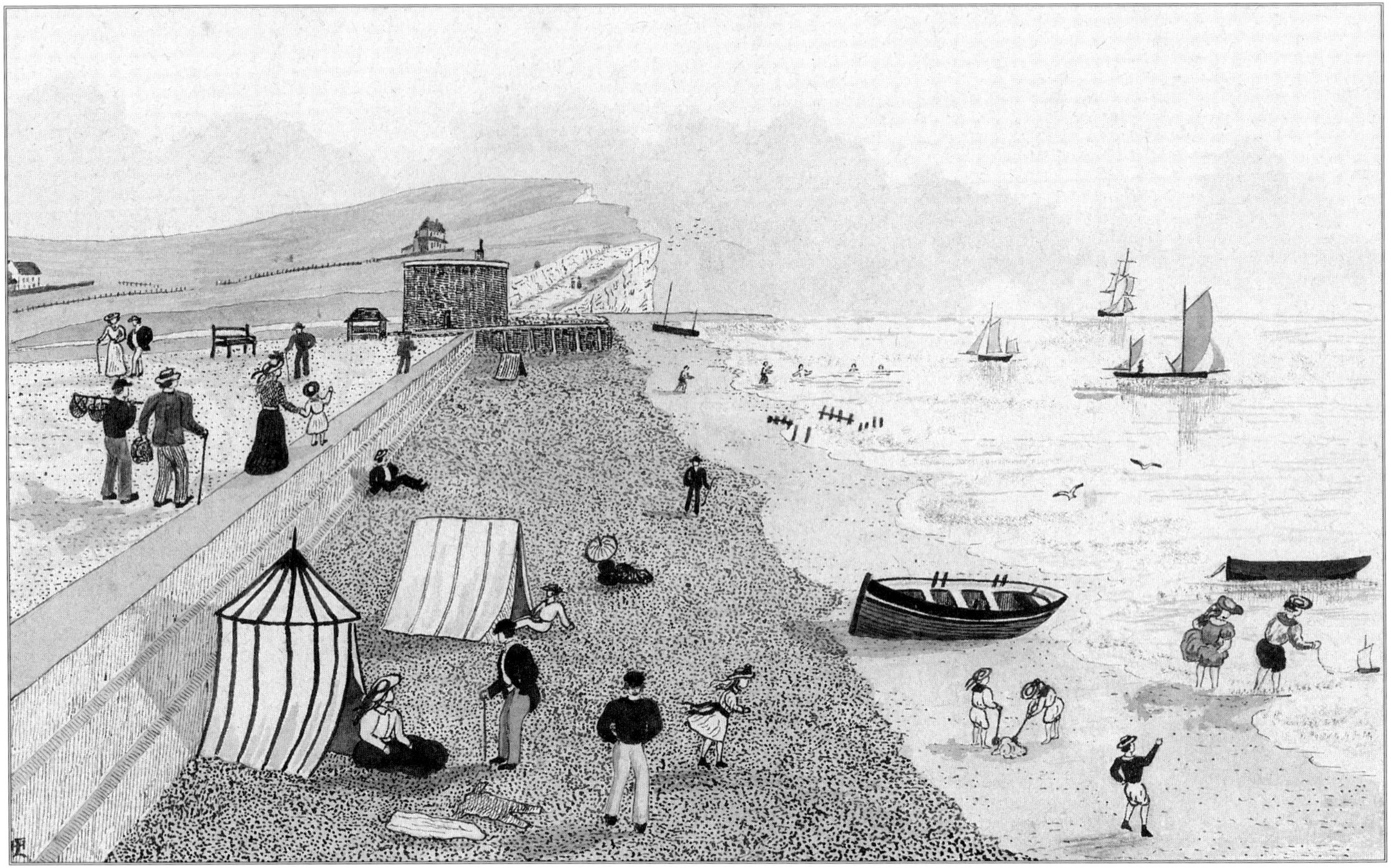

THE BEACH, — LOOKING EAST.

The beach looking east. The Martello Tower can be seen without its gun and without rendering on its walls.
The hotel on the cliffs can be seen above Splash Point.
(Size of original drawing 145 x 220mm)

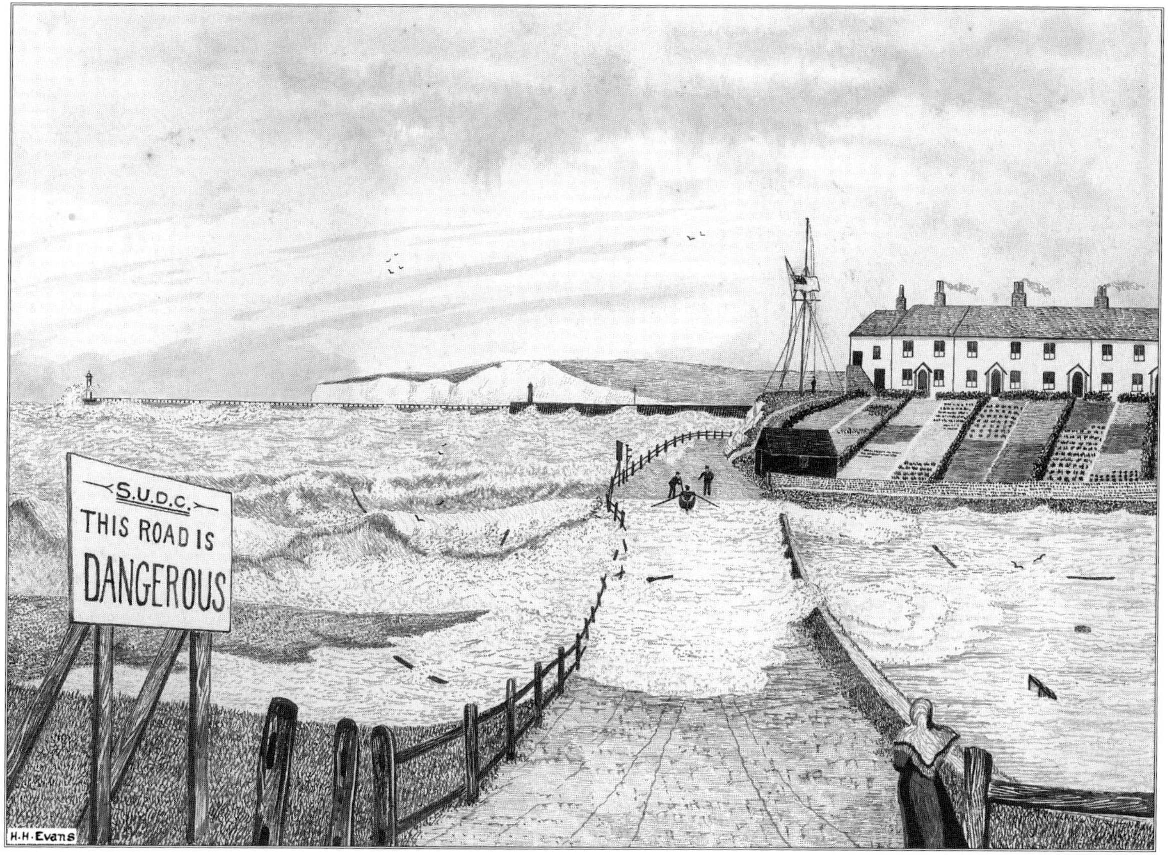

BUCKLE ROAD,
OCTOBER 9th 1896.

The most westerly of the drawings in this collection. The coast road was the main road out of Seaford and as it was frequently impassable at high tide it was the responsibility of the landlord of the Buckle Inn to put out warning notices. When Grand Avenue was built in the 1930's it became possible to take an alternative route via Blatchington and thence into the town. The Buckle by-pass was opened in the 1960's and the old road from the end of Grand Avenue to the top of Blatchington Hill is now only a footpath, having been superseded by housing estate roads. (Size of original drawing 155 x 210mm)

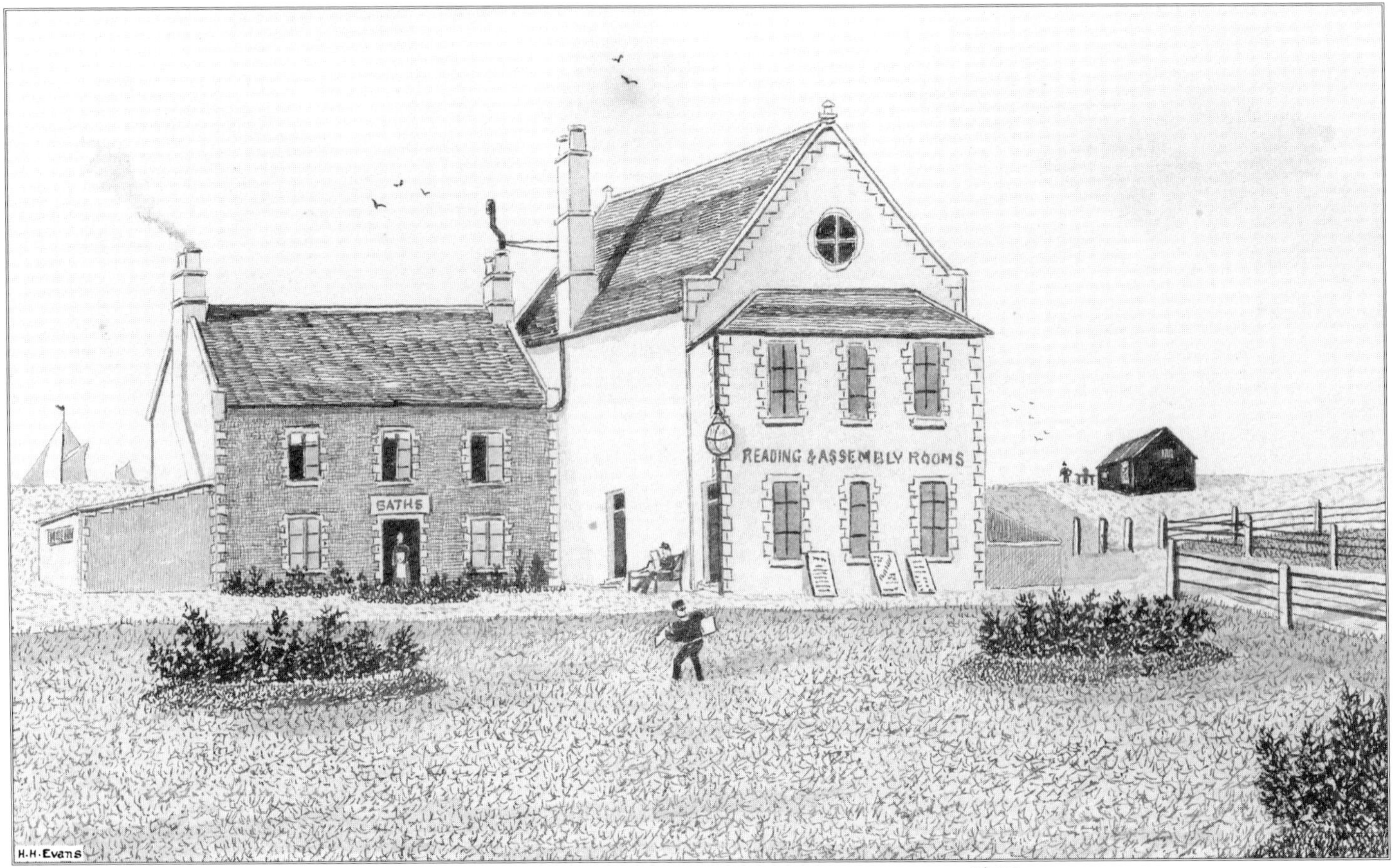

THE ASSEMBLY ROOMS BUILT BY DR TYLER SMITH 1870.
PULLED DOWN IN 1890 AND ESPLANADE HOTEL BUILT.

The Assembly Rooms and Baths were built by Dr Tyler-Smith and his committee in an effort to make Seaford a fashionable resort but the life of the rooms was short-lived. The Esplanade Hotel built on the site was briefly fashionable enjoying royal patronage upon occasion. It was demolished in its turn during the 1980's. (Size of original drawing 96 x 140mm)

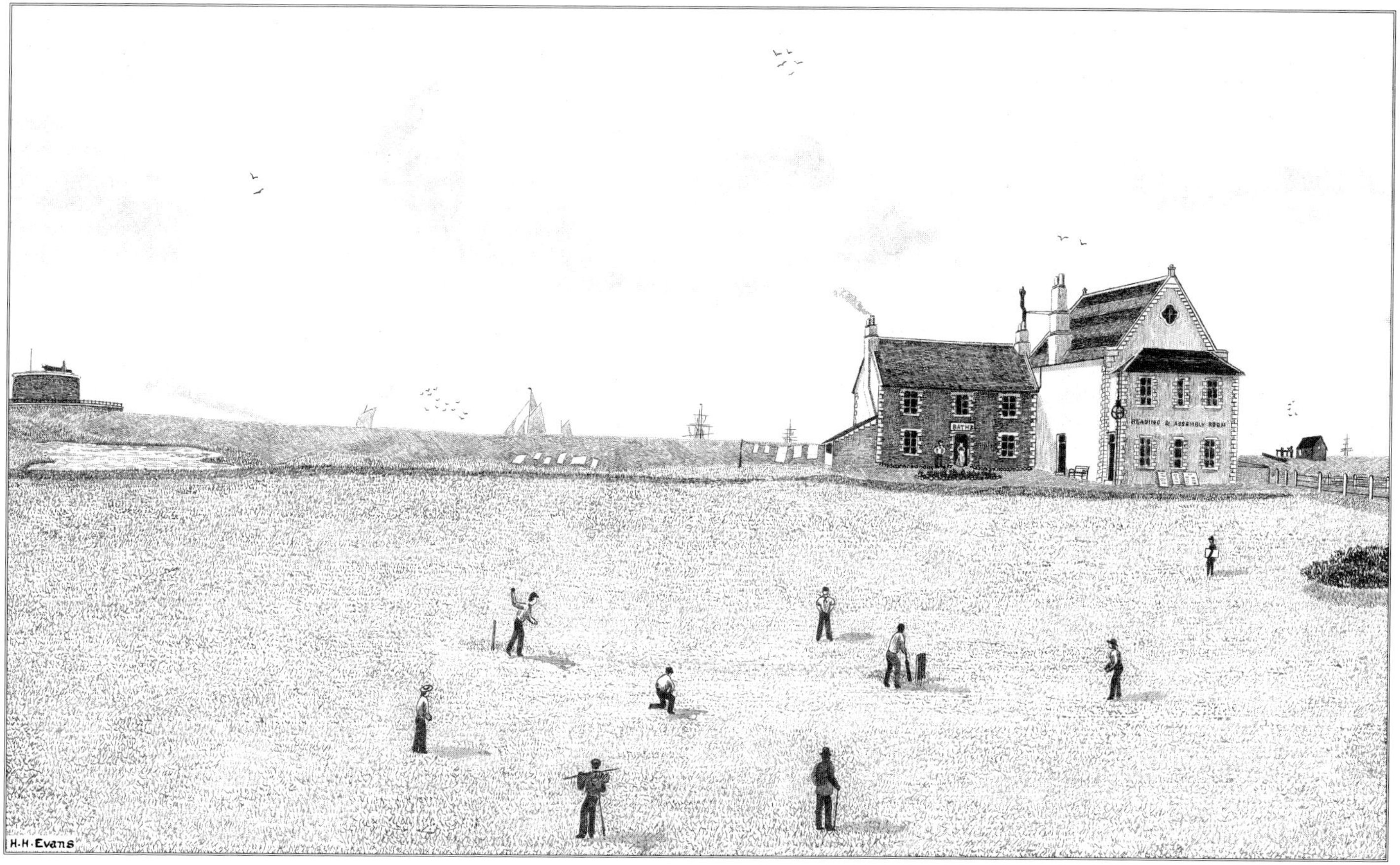

Baths and Assembly Rooms,
PULLED DOWN IN 1890, Esplanade Hotel STANDS ON SITE.

The Assembly Rooms and Baths from the landward side showing a cricket match taking place on the Cricketfield and Common. This open space was given to the town by Elizabeth I. The Martello Tower can be seen to the left of the drawing.
(Size of original drawing 195 x 295mm)

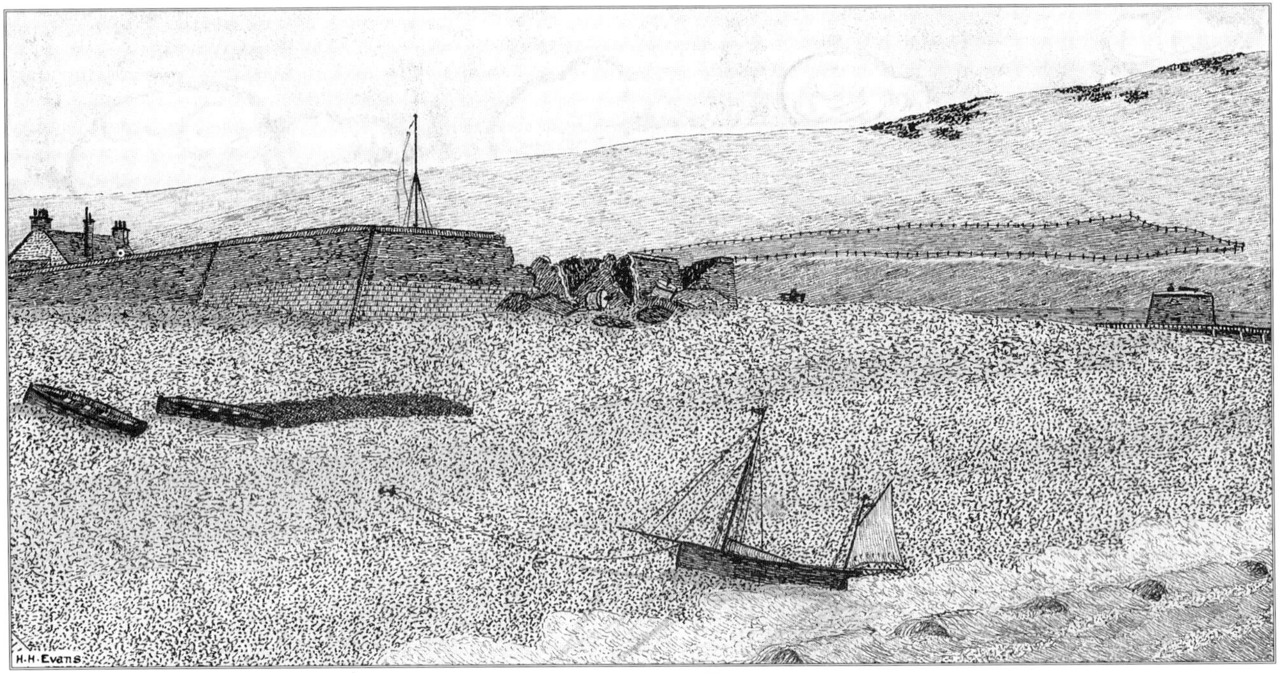

THE BATTERY AT SEAFORD.

After the great gale of 1875.

This Battery which stood in front of the present Esplanade Hotel mounted 4 guns, (68 & 32) pounders, and had accommodation for 2 Officers & 50 men. It was greatly damaged in the inundation of 1865 and again in the great storm & flood of 1875. Soon after this it was sold & broken up. The Jubilee drinking fountain in the Steine stands on one of the granite gun mounts.

There were two defensive batteries on the seafront. The Seaford Battery was close to the Assembly Rooms and the Martello Tower can be seen to the right of the picture. The other battery was known as the Blatchington Battery and was much further west.

(Size of original drawing 175 x 180mm)

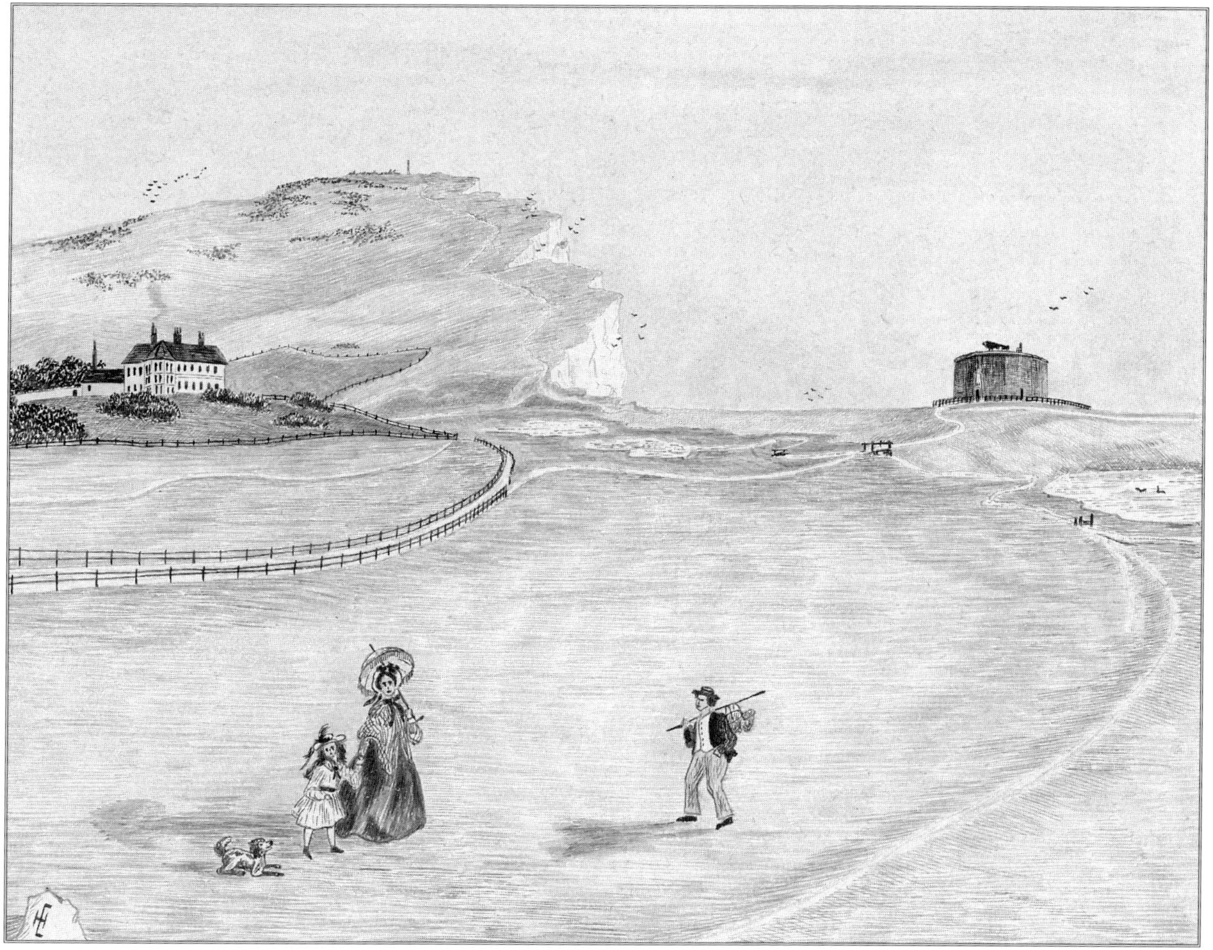

Corsica Hall and the Martello Tower. It is possible to see remnants of the old harbour, which were still in evidence until late in the 19th century.
(Size of original drawing 115 x 150mm)

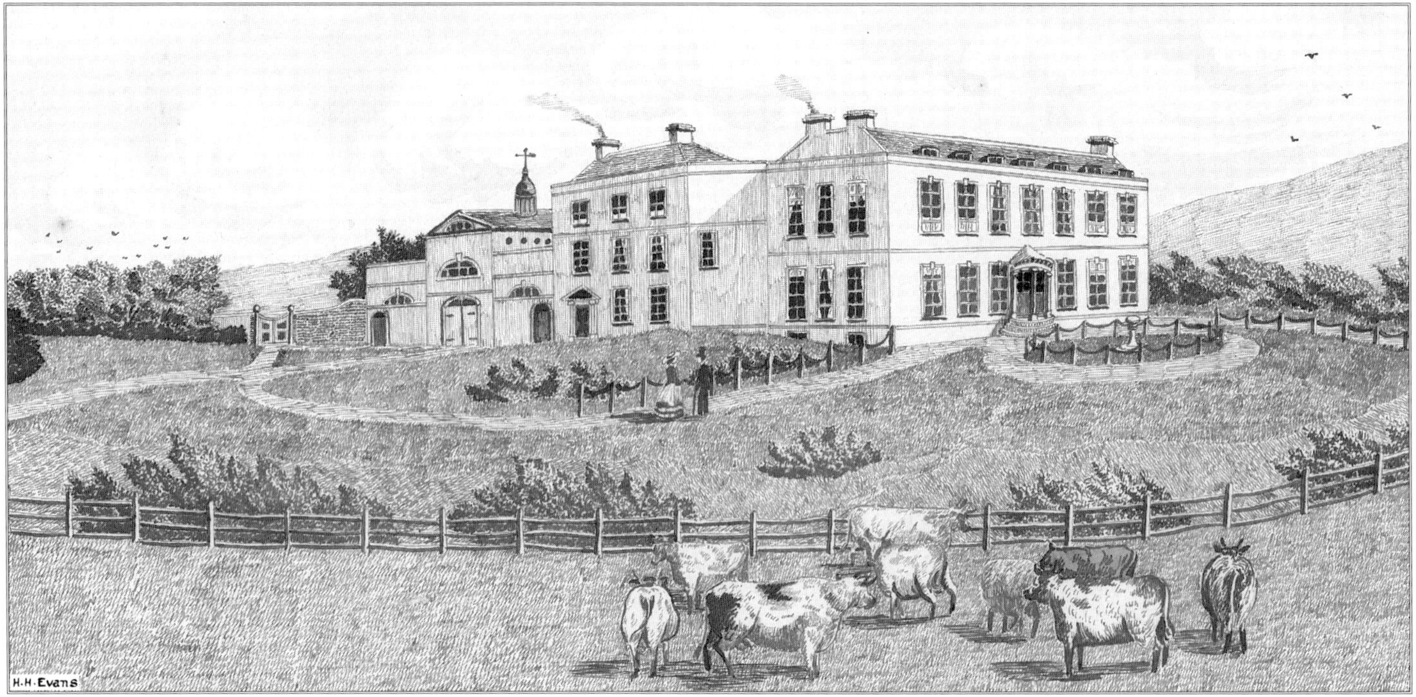

MILLBURG NOW SEAFORD COLLEGE

Millburg, the property of John Purcell Fitzgerald Esq., has the aliases of "Corsica Hall" and "The Lodge". The house was originally built by a person named Whitfield, who was a great smuggler of Corsican wine, whence the name Corsica Hall. A mill formerly stood here, whence the name, and some cannon occupied this commanding position. It was at one time the property of Francis, fifth Lord Napier, and in May 1772, became the scene of a painful domestic tragedy.

Corsica Hall was a nickname for this building, which was called Millburgh from its location on a small hill on which there was once a mill. The nickname has now become the formal name of the building but was derived originally from the first owner whose source of income was thought to be smuggled Corsican wines. The home of Seaford College from its foundation until its move to Midhurst during World War Two, Corsica Hall has been used for a variety of educational activities and is currently a field-study and conference centre.

(Size of original drawing 175 x 230mm)

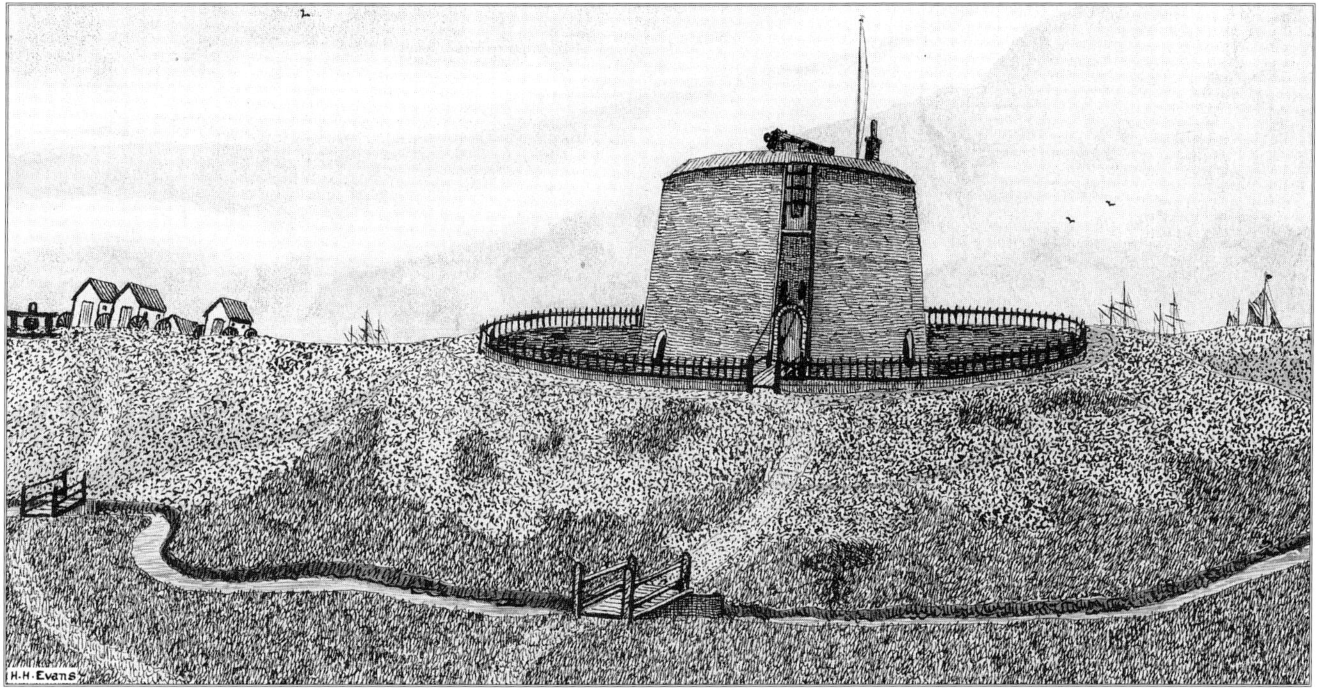

THE MARTELLO TOWER, No 74. SEAFORD.

From the grounds Corsica Hall.

It cost £18,000, and contains room for one officer and 24 men, fitted with four fire and damp proof magazines, and one 64 pounder gun. Surrounded by a deep moat which can be flooded at will, crossed by iron drawbridge, which when drawn up completely covers door and entrance. Was dismantled in 1882, when lowering the gun the tackle slip'd the gun fell into the moat carrying away the bridge.

The tower ditch connected two large saltwater ponds, one in front of the town the other near the Cliff end. It is now used (after great alteration) for public Teas, baths, skatingrink &c. &c.

The Martello Tower from the landward side showing the gun on the roof and the drawbridge. (Size of original drawing 190 x 180mm)

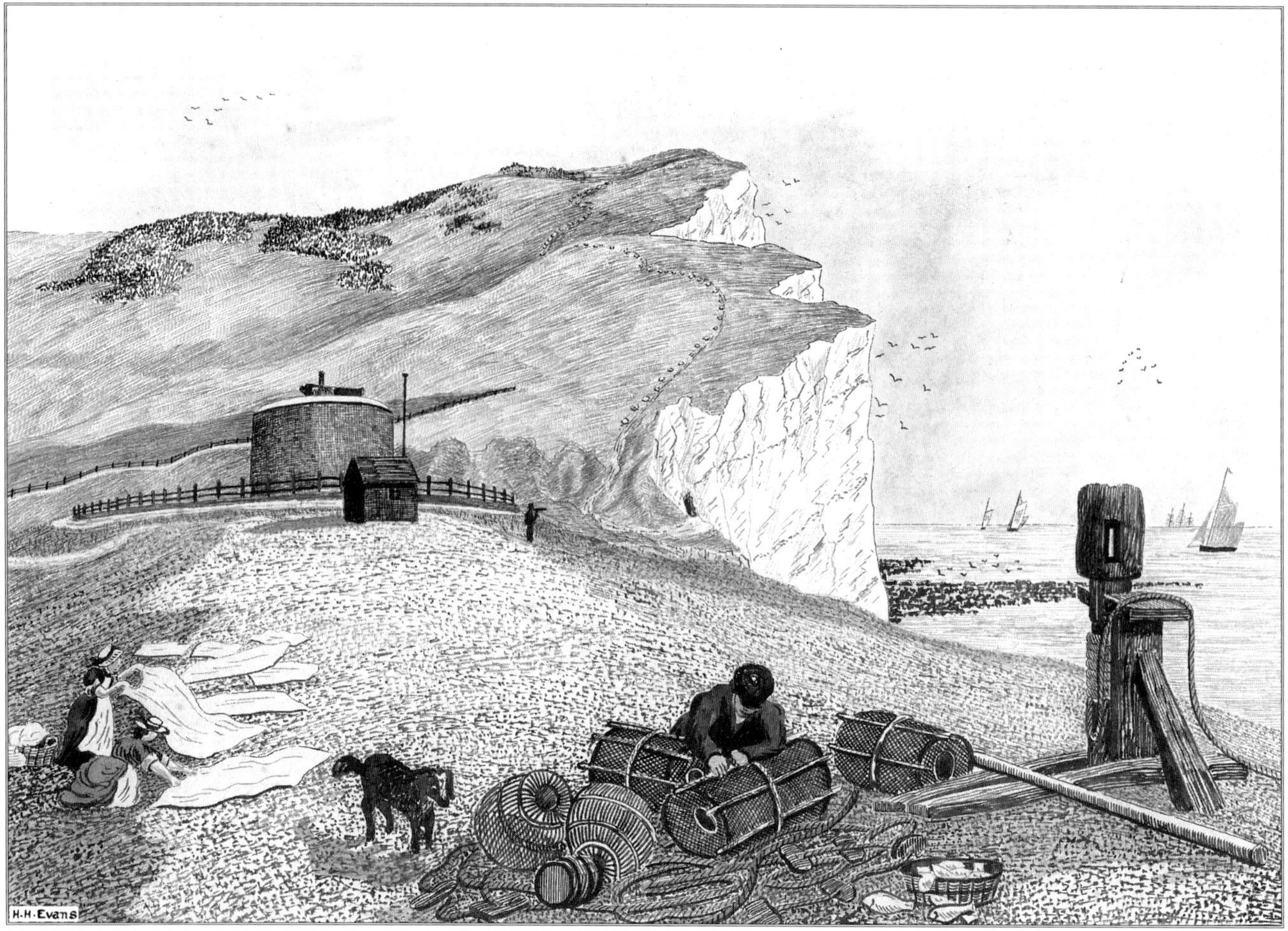

SEAFORD CLIFF & MARTELLO TOWER. 1868.
From an Oil Painting.

The cliffs and Martello Tower from an oil painting by W Collins (1788 - 1847). Note the laundry drying on the beach and also the line of stones to mark the dangerous cliff edge over Seaford Head. (Size of original drawing 160 x 210mm)

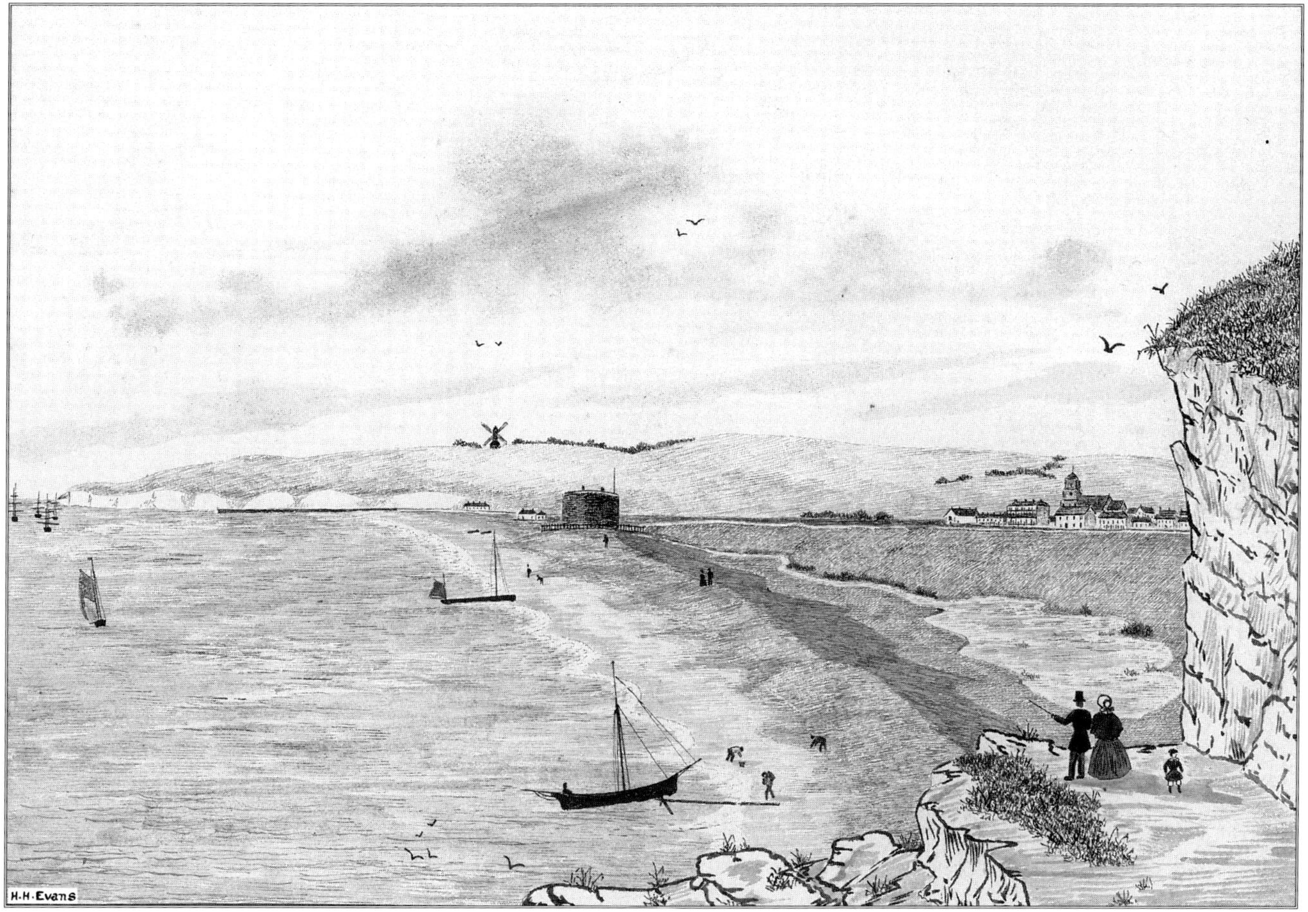

SEAFORD BAY.
FROM A DRAWING 1821

Looking west from Splash Point over Seaford Bay from an 1821 drawing. (Origin unknown at present) The sea wall had yet to be built and the remnants of the harbour are clearly seen. The windmill in the distance appears to be above Newhaven.

(Size of original drawing 160 x 210mm)

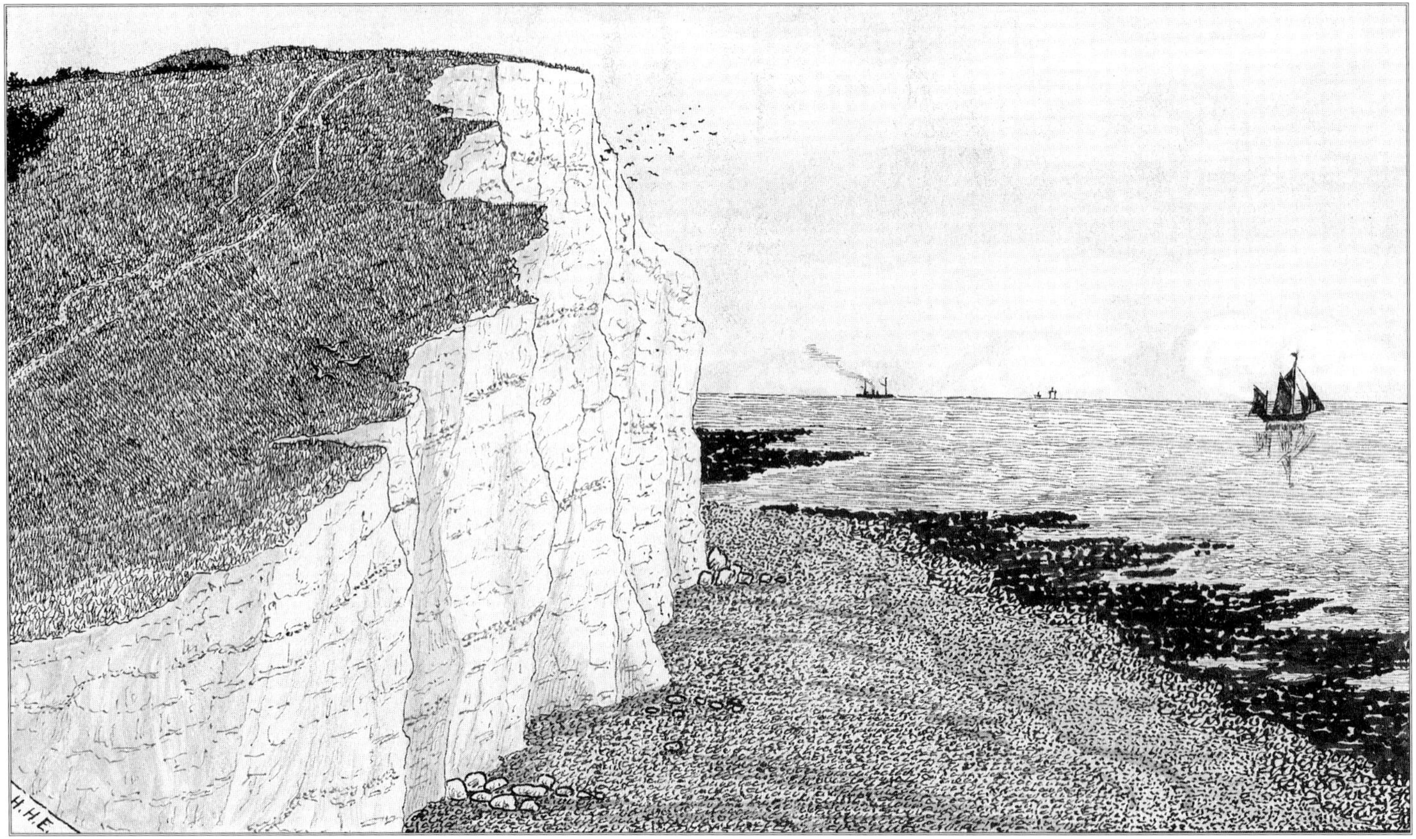

THE CLIFFS AT SEAFORD.

Seaford Head rises to a height of 302 feet of pure white chalk above the level of the sea.
These rocks are a favorite prawning ground.

Seaford Head from Splash Point. The shape of the cliffs change from year to year due to erosion. (Size of original drawing 160 x 180mm)

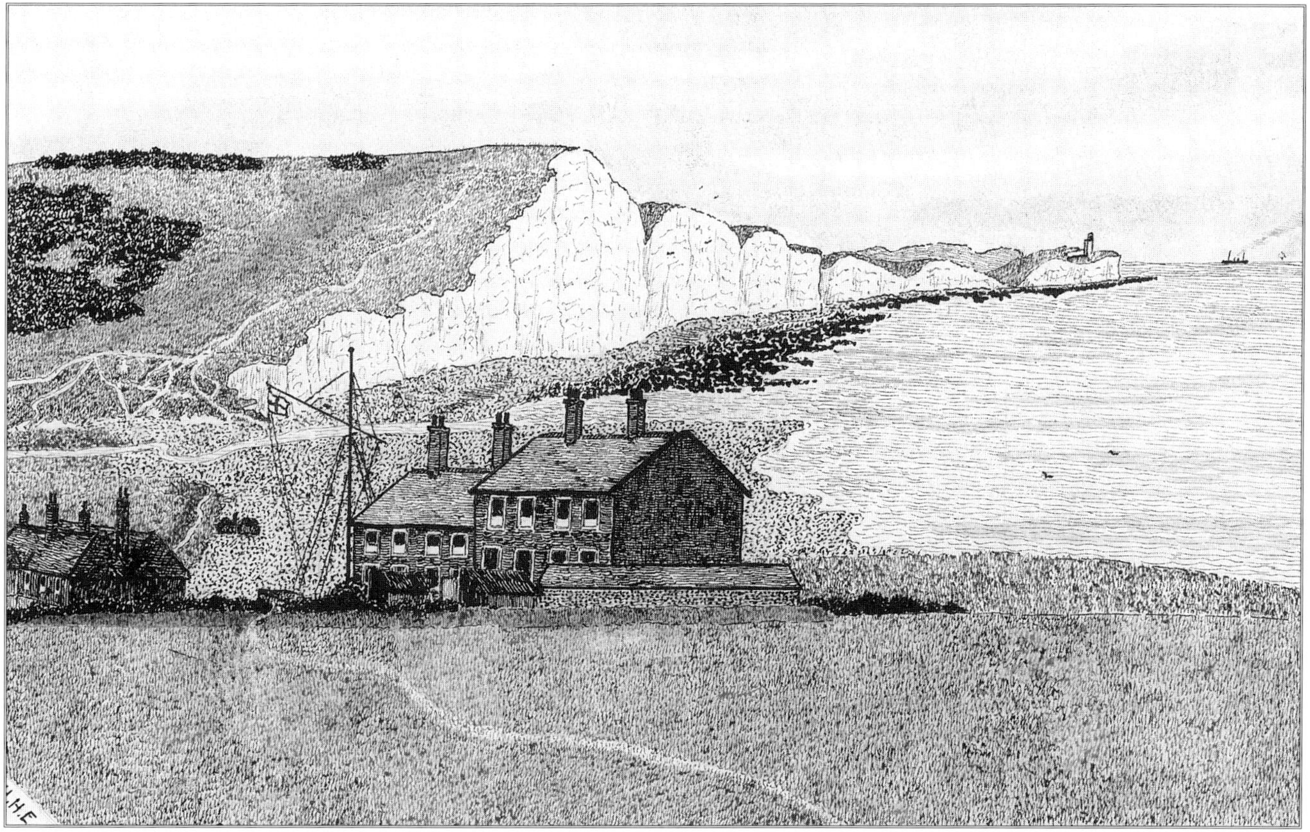

THE COASTGUARD STATION, CUCKMERE.

A wireless telegraph station was erected on the lefthand side of the chiefboatmans house in 1914 for communication during the war. It is still used and a staff kept at the station.

The Coastguard Cottages above Cuckmere Haven, showing the Seven Sisters and Belle Tout lighthouse in the right background.
(Size of original drawing 160 x 180mm)

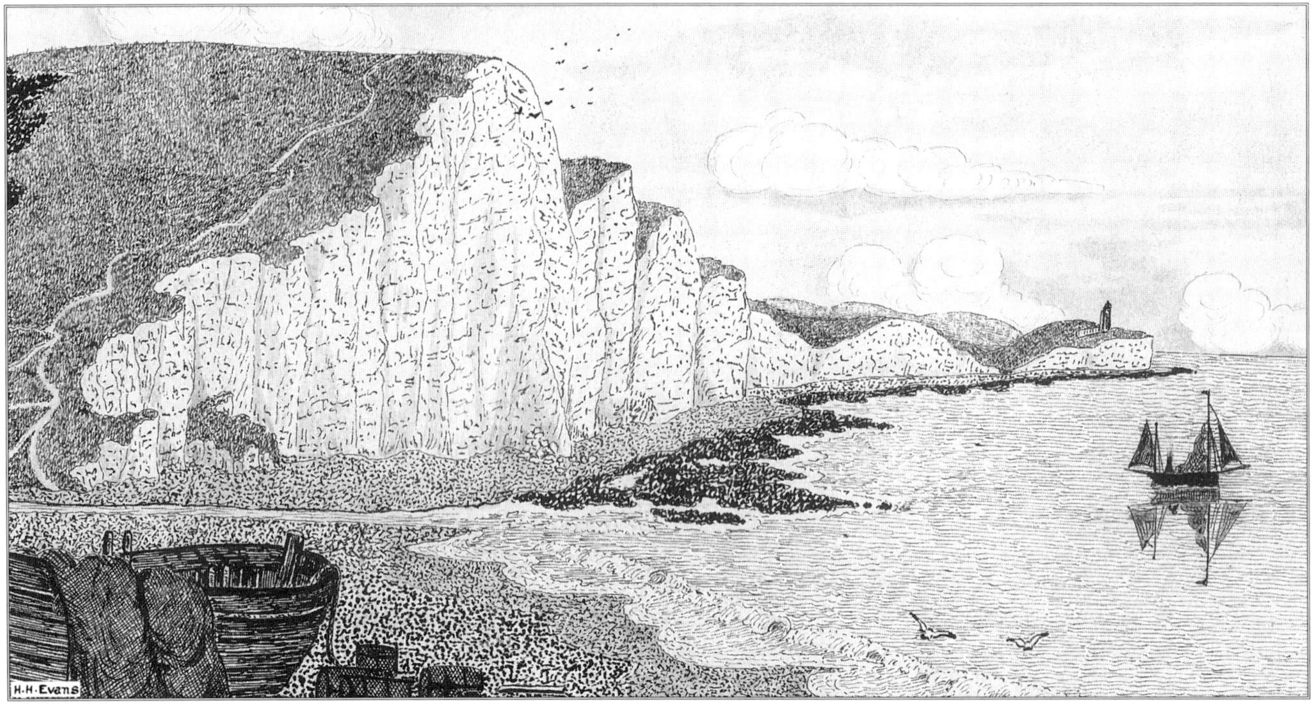

THE SEVEN SISTERS AND BEL'TOUTE LIGHTHOUSE.
From the beach at Cuckmere.

Belle Toute lighthouse is now a private residence. The new lighthouse under Beachy head occupied nearly three years building and was completed towards the end of 1902. It is built of blocks of Cornish granite, is circular, and of the same pattern as the well known Eddystone. The foundation is sunk 18 feet into the solid chalk each block weighing four to five tons. The diamiter is 30 feet at the base, and the height 140 feet. It stands on the rocks, about 500 yards from the cliff.

A further view of the Seven Sisters from the beach at Cuckmere Haven. (Size of original drawing 185 x 180mm)

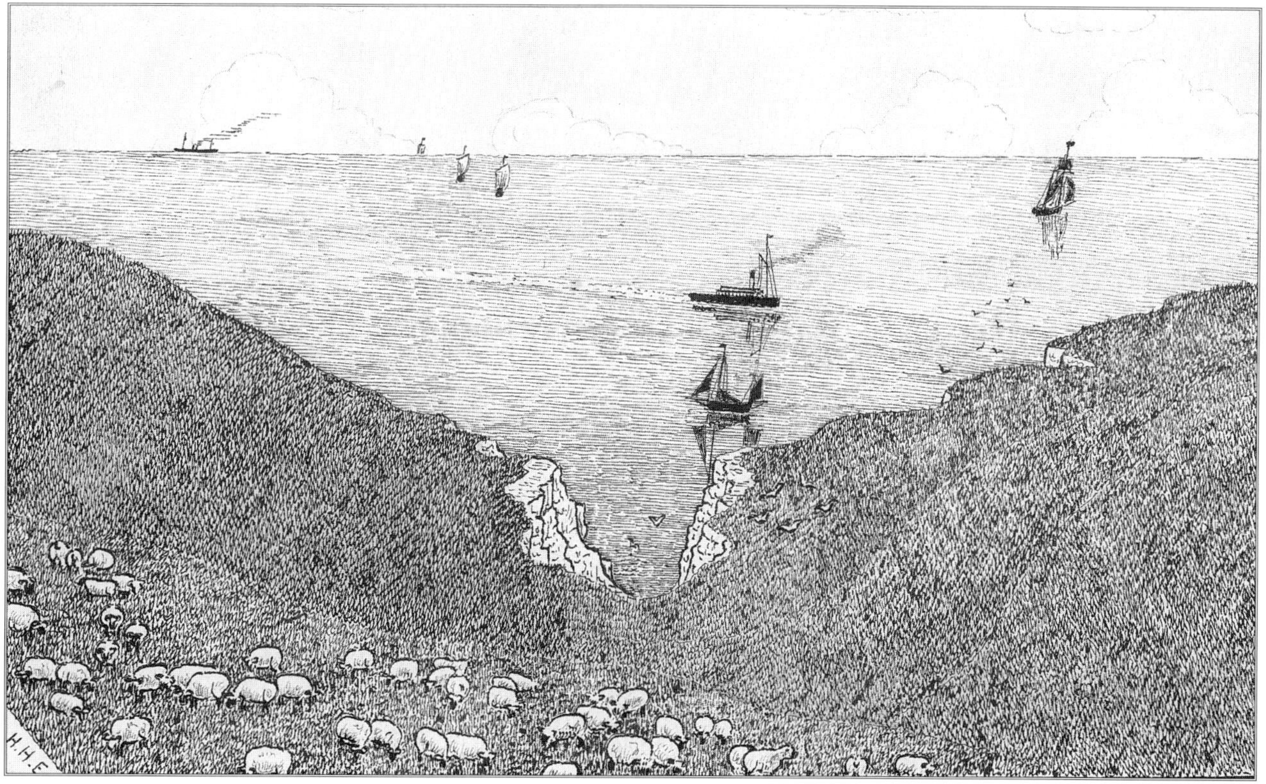

PUCK CHURCH NEAR SEAFORD

This gap formerly went down to the beach. There were also two large caves on either side, called Pucks' parlours, connected from the top of the cliff by a narrow and dangerous path. The last man to enter them was Tom Cheal, who went down with a rope to get three young Peregrine falcons in 1881.

Puck Church was a gap in the cliff between Seaford Head and Hope Gap.
The drawing has a description of the gap with caves below and of the rescue of three peregrine falcons. (Size of original drawing 175 x 180mm)

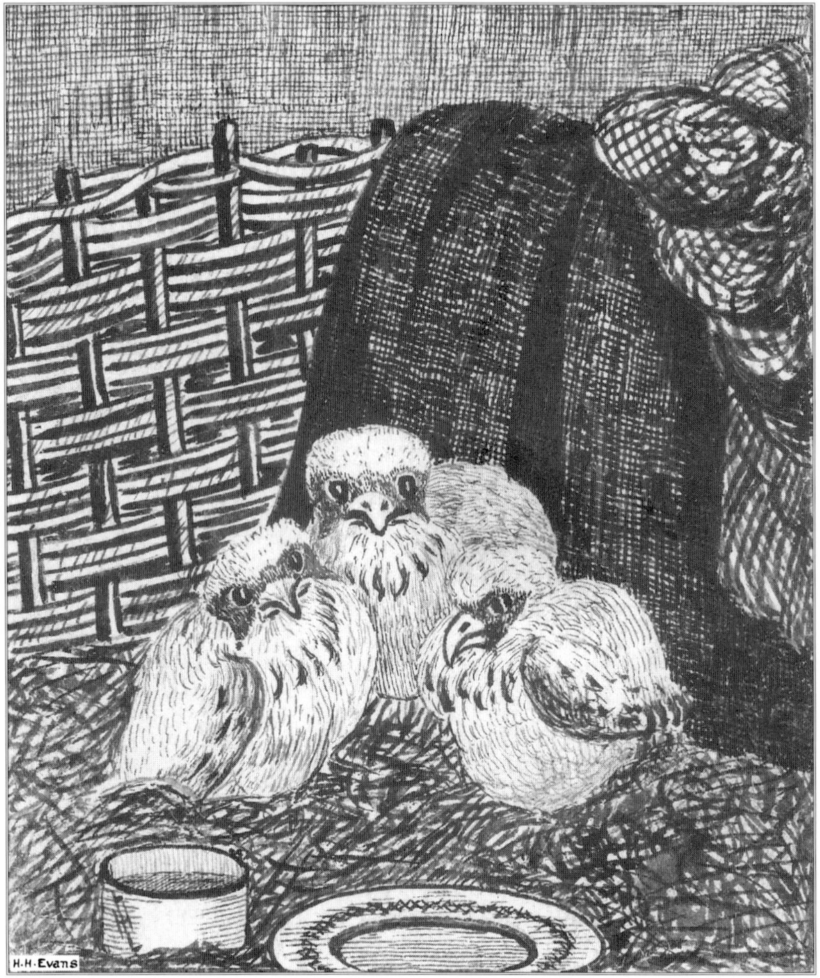

An unusual drawing of the rescued falcons.
(Size of original drawing 88 x 65mm)

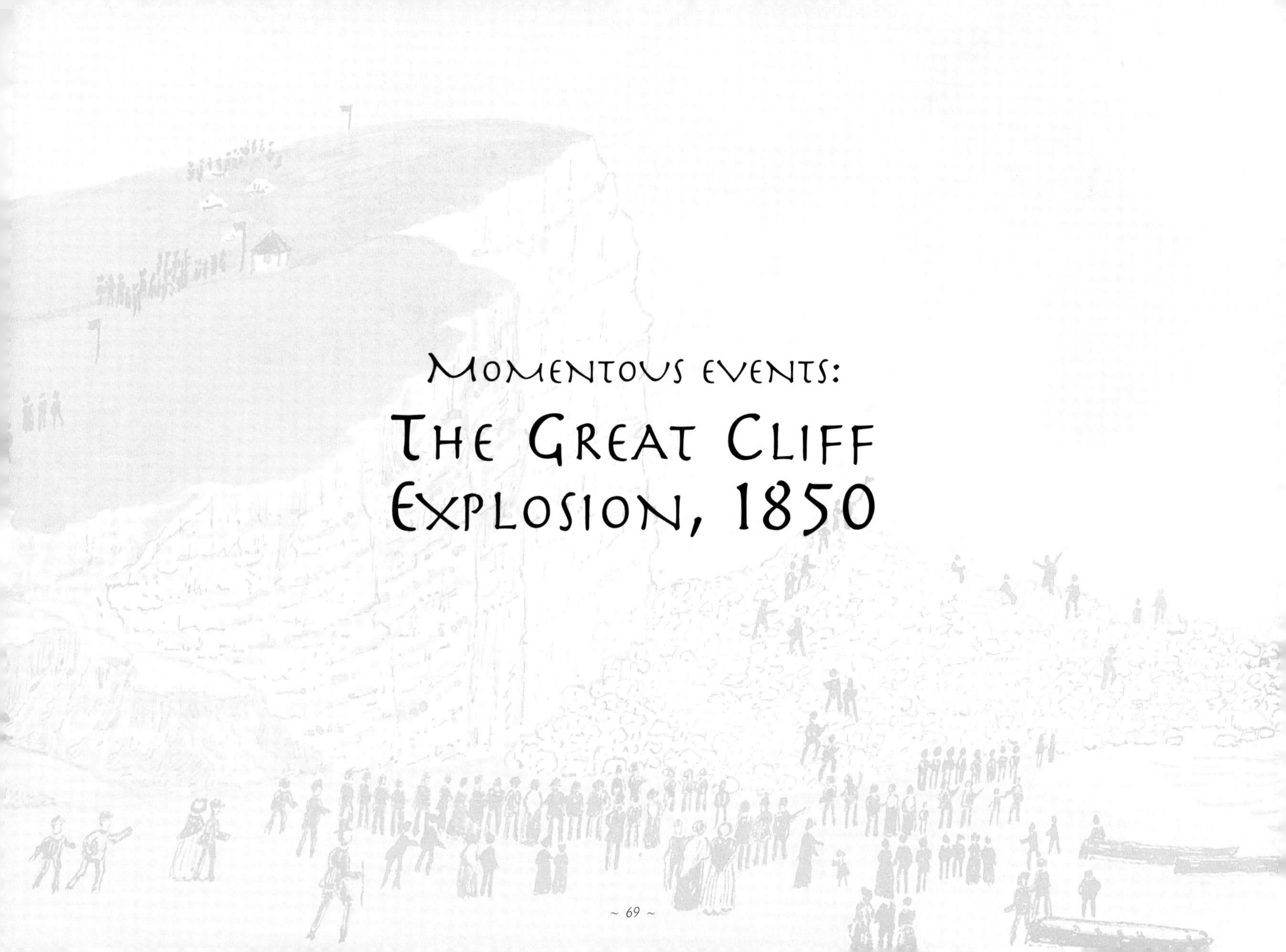

Momentous events: The Great Cliff Explosion, 1850

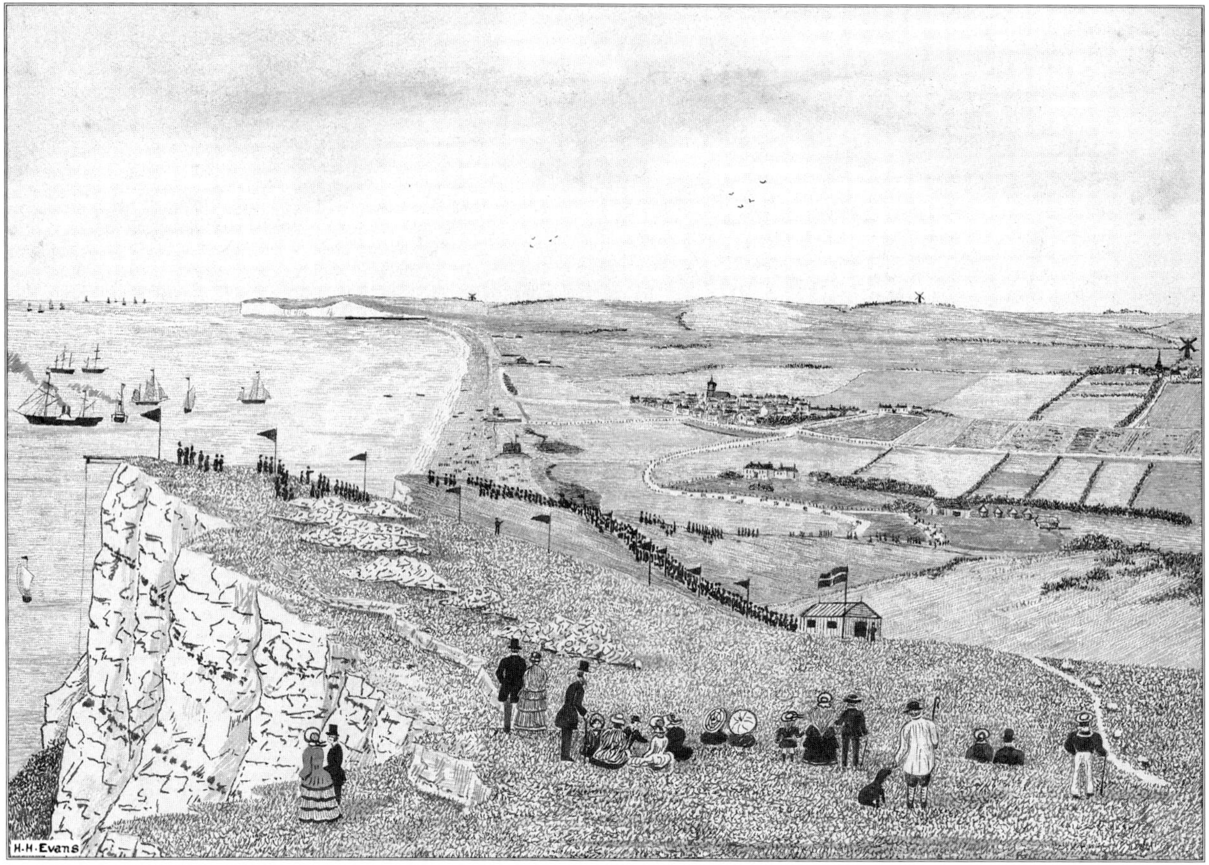

THE GREAT EXPLOSION AT SEAFORD 1850.

1850 saw the great explosion at Seaford when an attempt was made to prevent further erosion of the base of the cliffs by forming a barrier with chalk blasted from the cliff. The blast was so strong that the chalk powdered and was rapidly washed away. The event caused great interest and this drawing is a copy of a picture in The Illustrated London News of the day. Many well-known citizens came to watch including Charles Dickens, who must have known Evans' father as both served on the same committee.

(Size of original drawing 155 x 210mm)

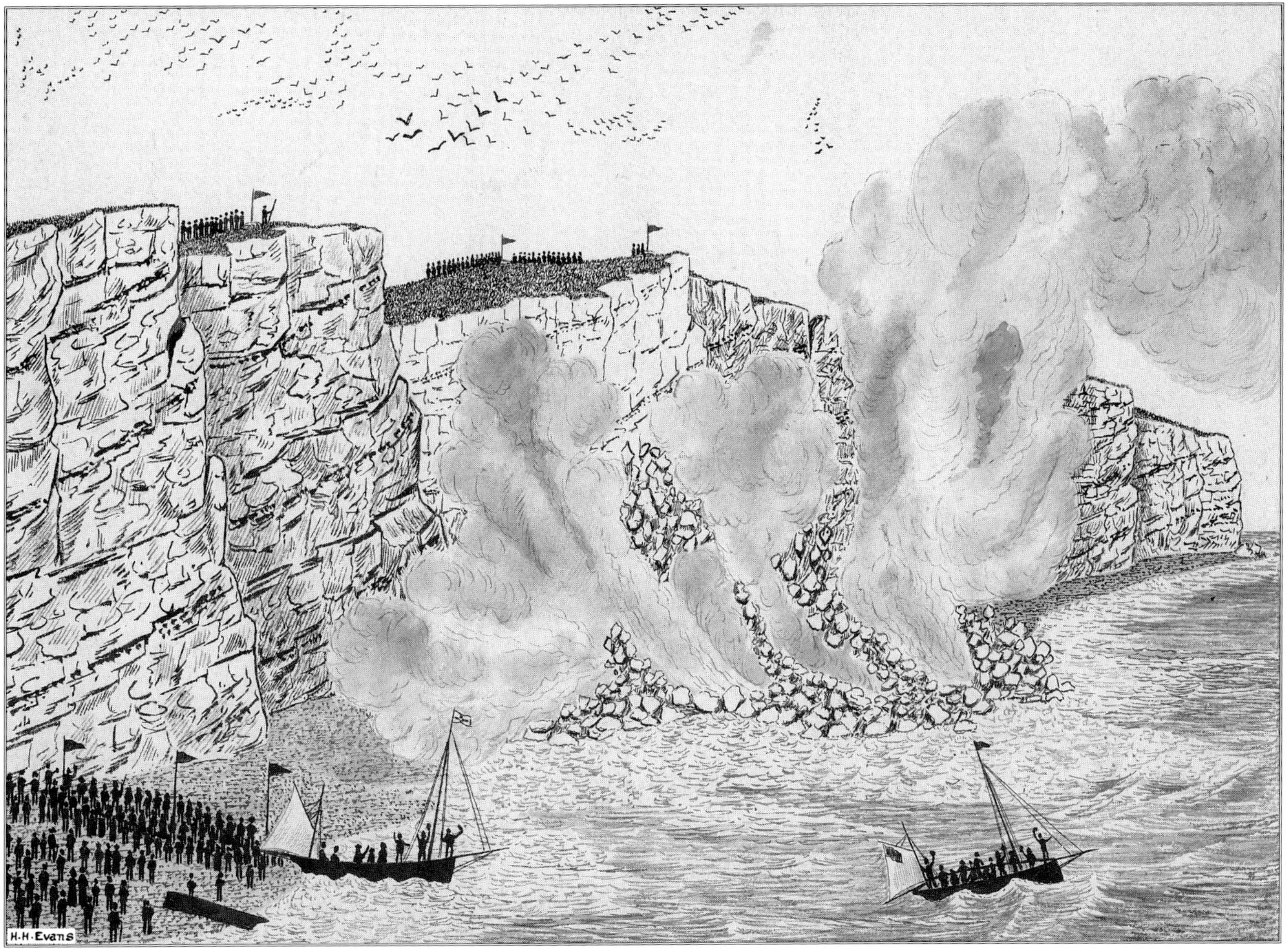

THE EXPLOSION 1850, CLIFF FALLING.

Drawing showing the cliff falling. Also copied from The Illustrated London News. (Size of original drawing 150 x 230mm)

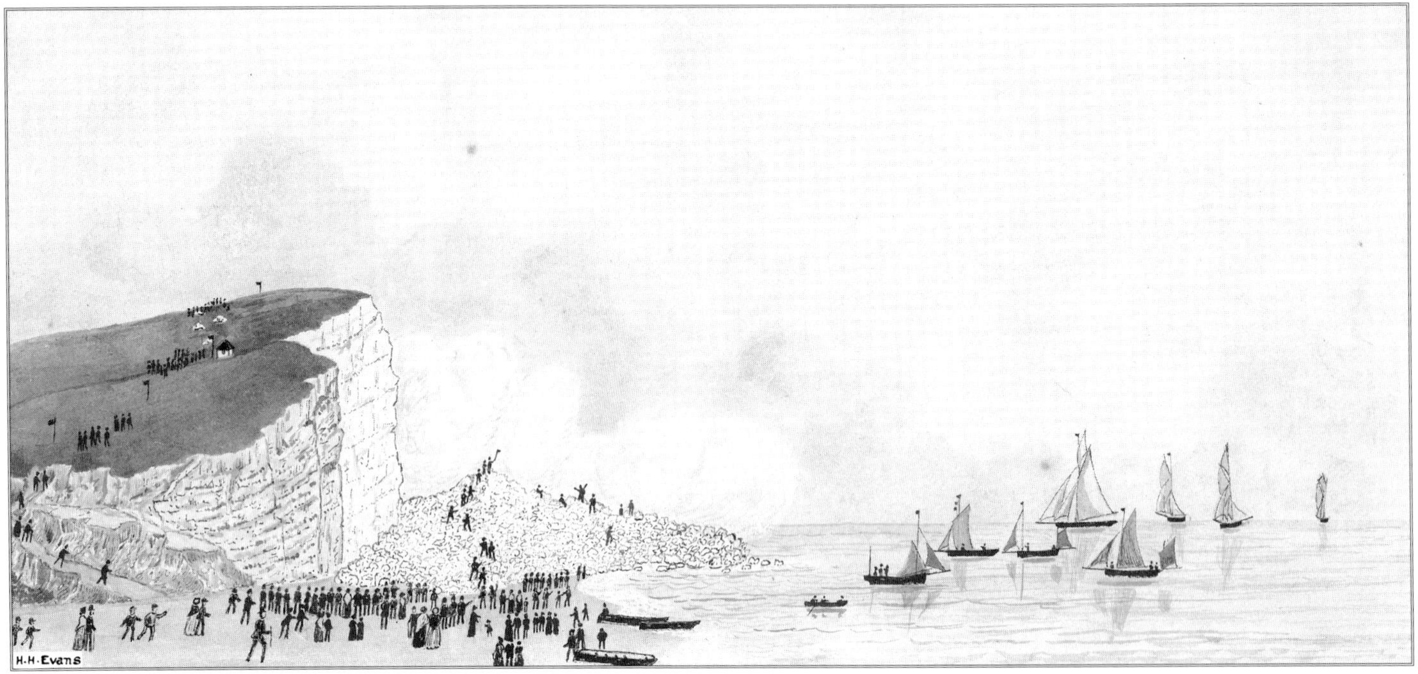

CLIFF EXPLOSION 1850.

In 1850, an attempt was made, by blasting an immense mass, of the chalk cliff into the sea, to form a kind, of rough groyne. The explosion, which was carried out by a body of Sappers and Miners, was successful enough, but too much gunpowder being used, the chalk, dislodged was reduced to small pieces, and the force of the tides soon swept away the enormous mole, which consisted of many thousands of tons; and all the expence and labour were lost. Mark Antony Lower, M.A., F.S.A, etc.

A view immediately after the explosion. Evans' notes are quoted from Mark Anthony Lower, a well-known Seaford historian. Note all the sightseers swarming over the chalk mound and the cliffs.

(Size of original drawing 160 x 275mm)

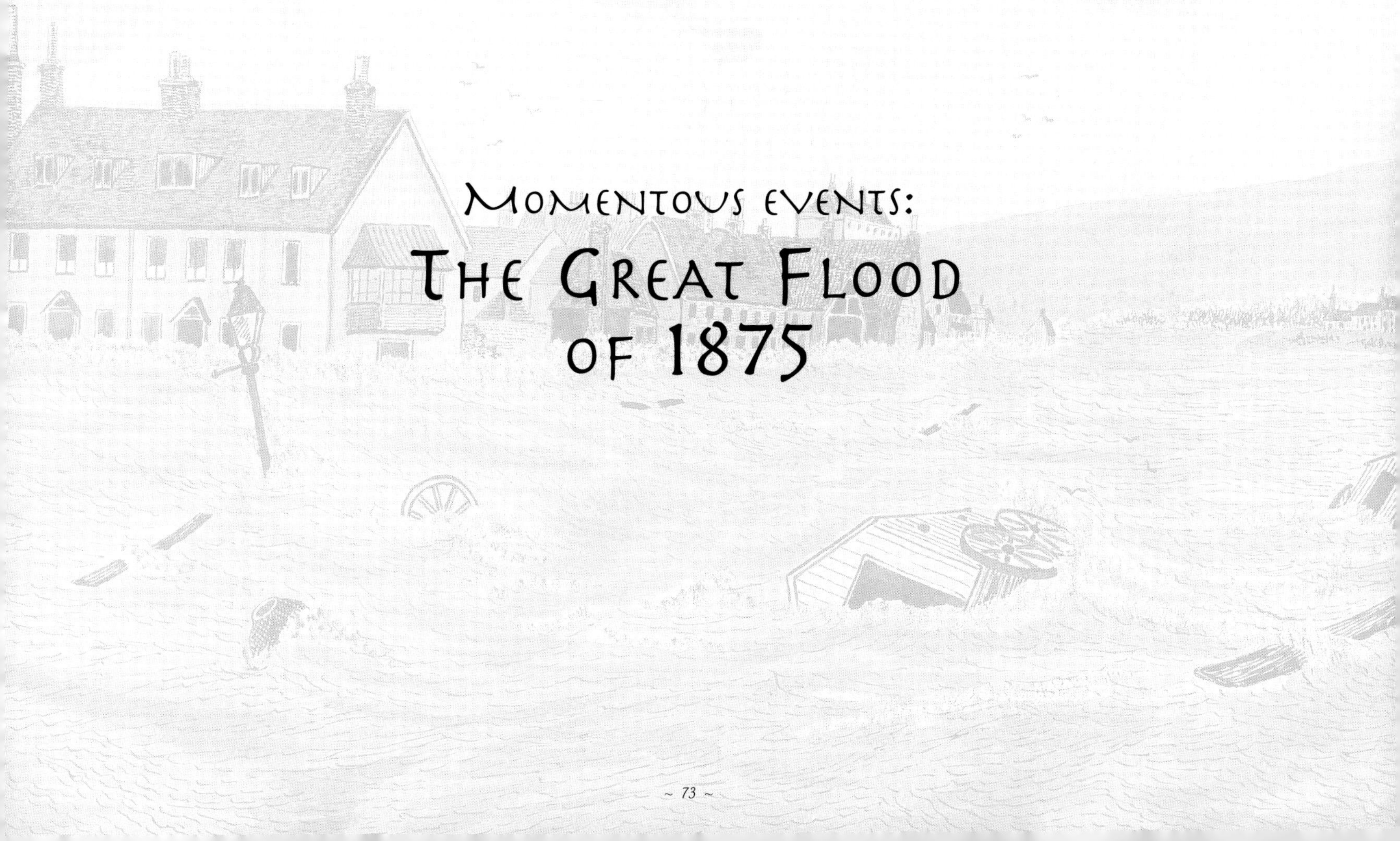

Momentous events:

The Great Flood of 1875

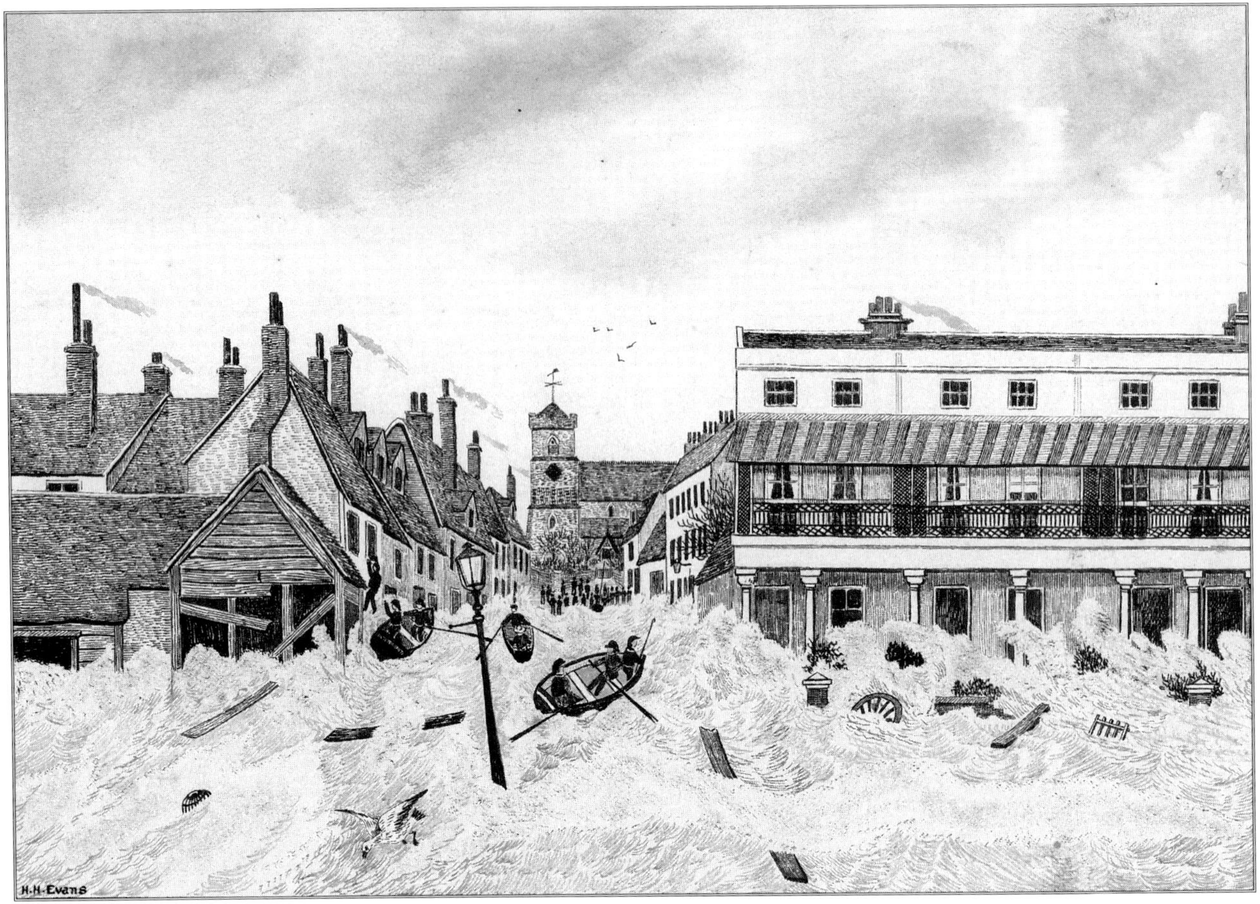

THE FLOOD 1875 CHURCH ST.

BOATS TO THE RESCUE.

This was one of the worst floods ever recorded in Seaford and happened before the building of the sea wall in 1881. The sea reached the church gate and in this drawing figures can be seen standing outside the church, watching other people being rescued from first floor windows by boat. This drawing is taken from a painting by J Moxon. (Size of original drawing 160 x 210mm)

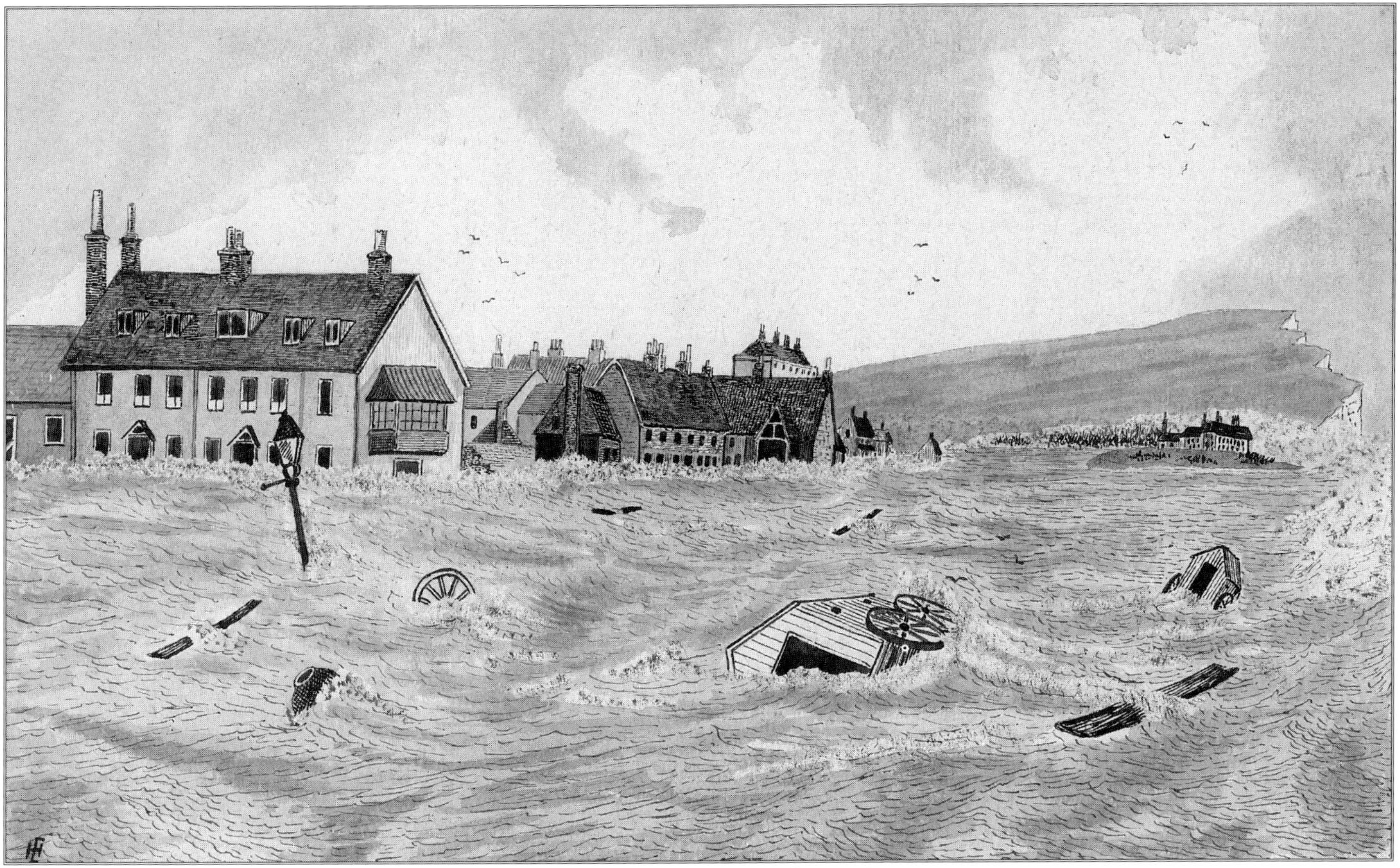

THE FLOOD, Sunday, November 14th 1875.
—Looking East.—

The view looking east. West House, Parliament Row and houses in the Steyne can be seen with Corsica Hall rising above the floods in the distance. In the foreground the remains of bathing machines and a lobster pot can be seen tossing about.
(Size of original drawing 155 x 255mm)

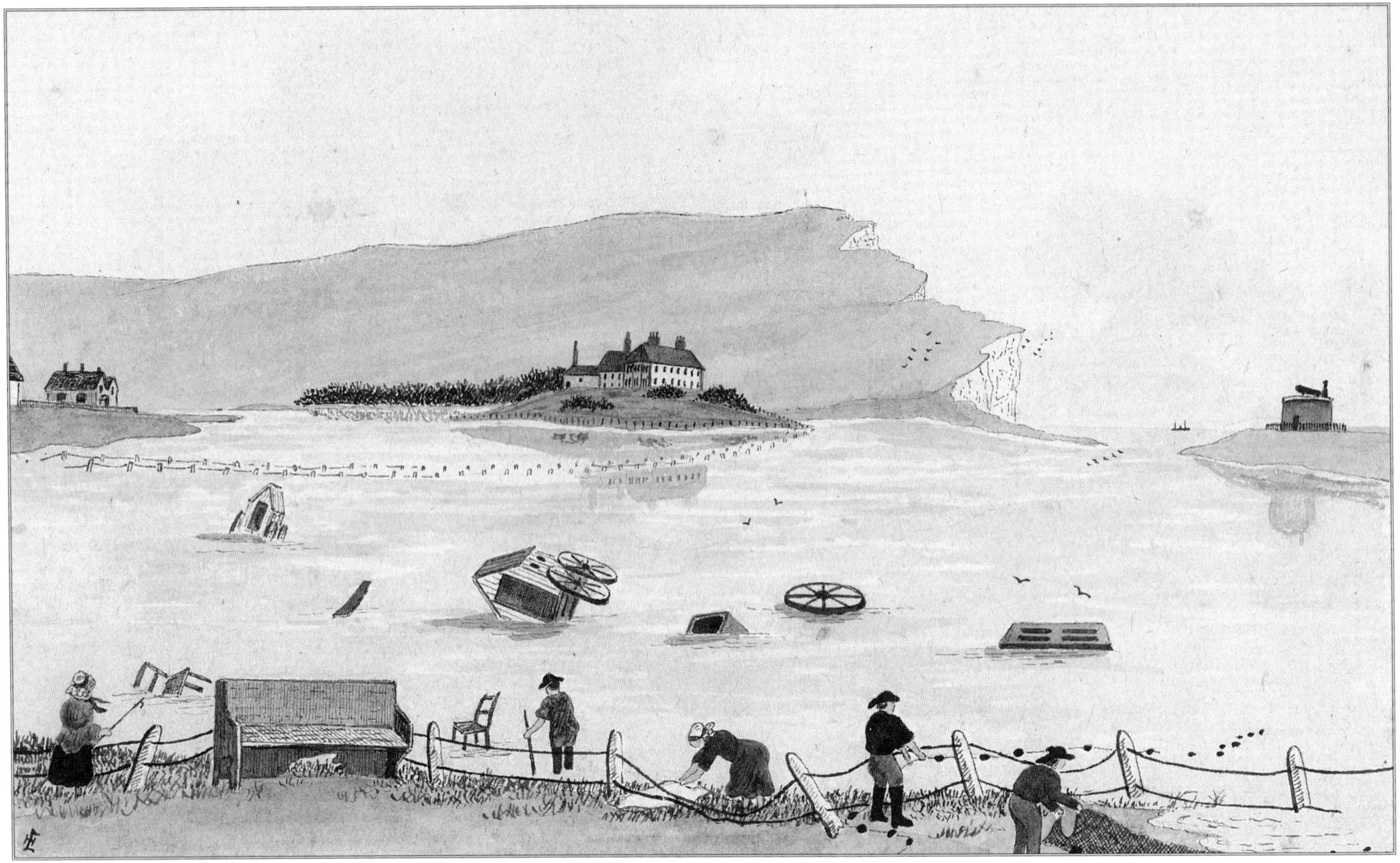

AFTER THE FLOOD, *from the Cawsway* {FLOTSAM & JETSAM}.

A more detailed view of the old harbour area showing it as it might have been in mediaeval times, except that where Corsica Hall stands there would have been a mill and the shingle bank would have been bare at that time.
(Size of original drawing 145 x 225mm)

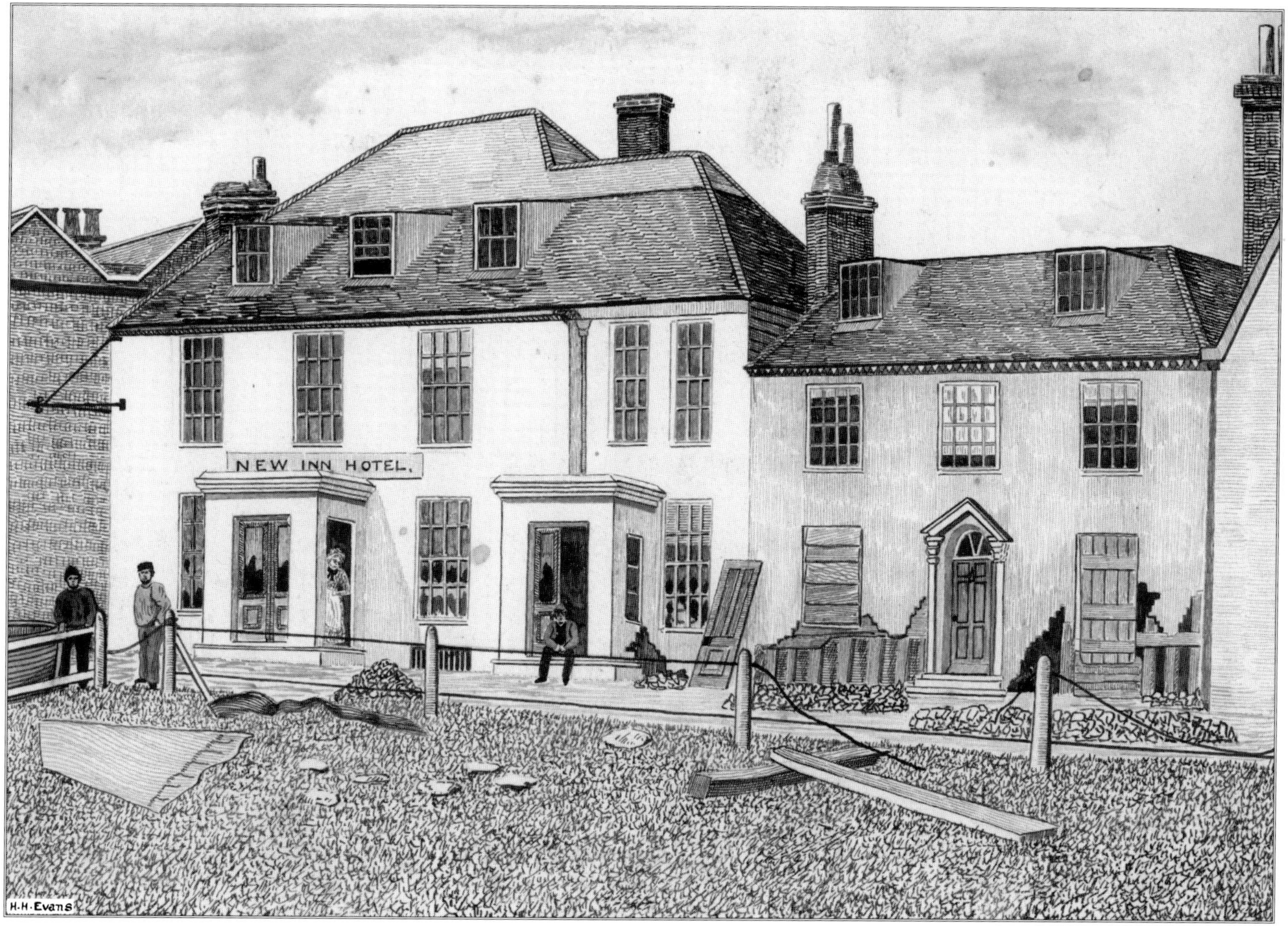

NEW INN HOTEL AND STEYNE HOUSE AFTER THE FLOOD NOV. 14th 1875.

The New Inn and Steyne House after the flood. Both buildings still exist.
(Size of original drawing 155 x 210mm)

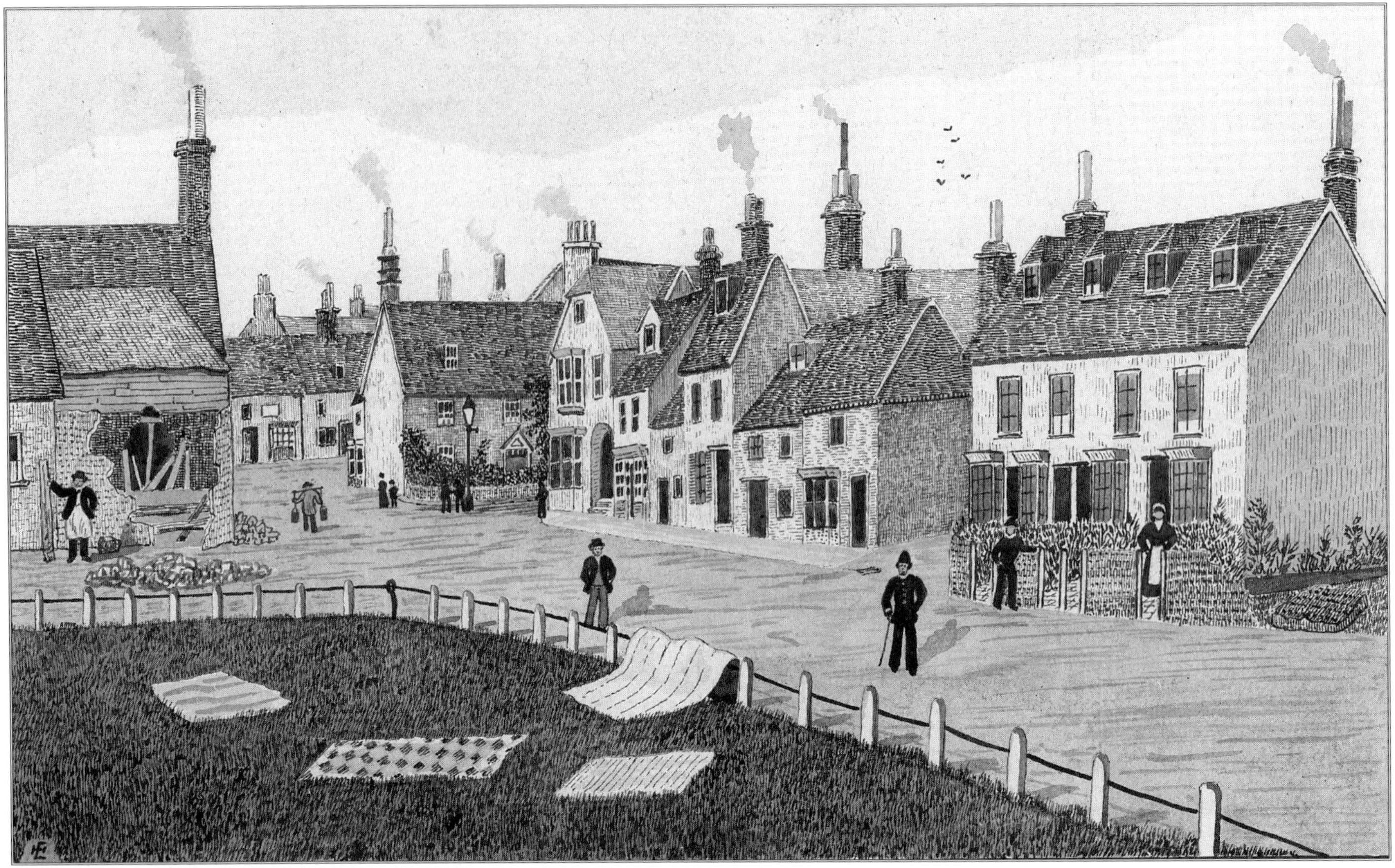

AFTER THE FLOOD, —— SOUTH STREET.

South Street showing damaged buildings. Evans' father retired to one of the cottages to the right of the picture.
Note the policeman with a walking stick who appears in many of Evans' drawings!
(Size of original drawing 145 x 225mm)

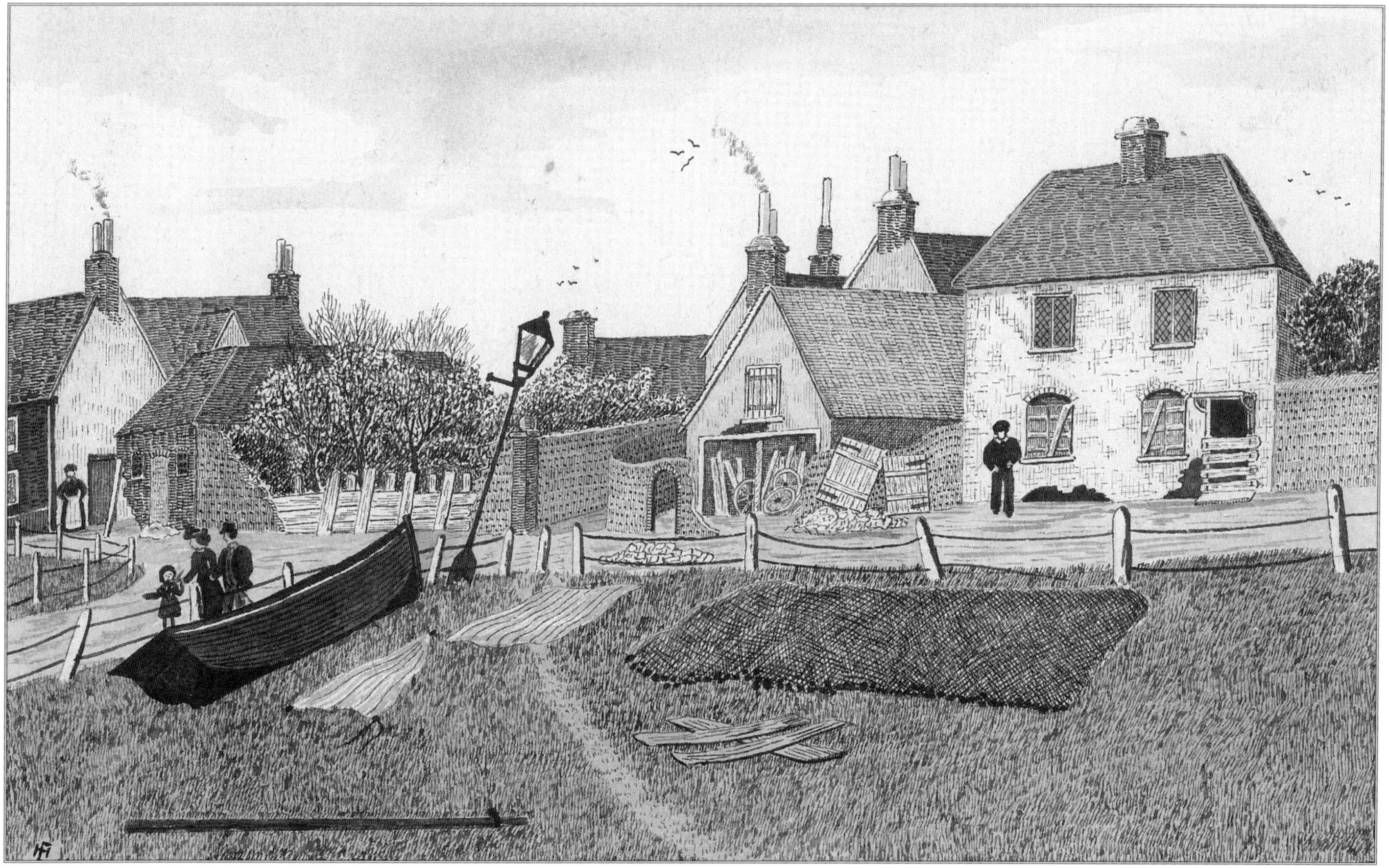

AFTER THE FLOOD, *BOTTOM OF DARK LANE, SOUTH ST*

The bottom end of Saxon Lane where the Barn Theatre now stands.
(Size of original drawing 145 x 225mm)

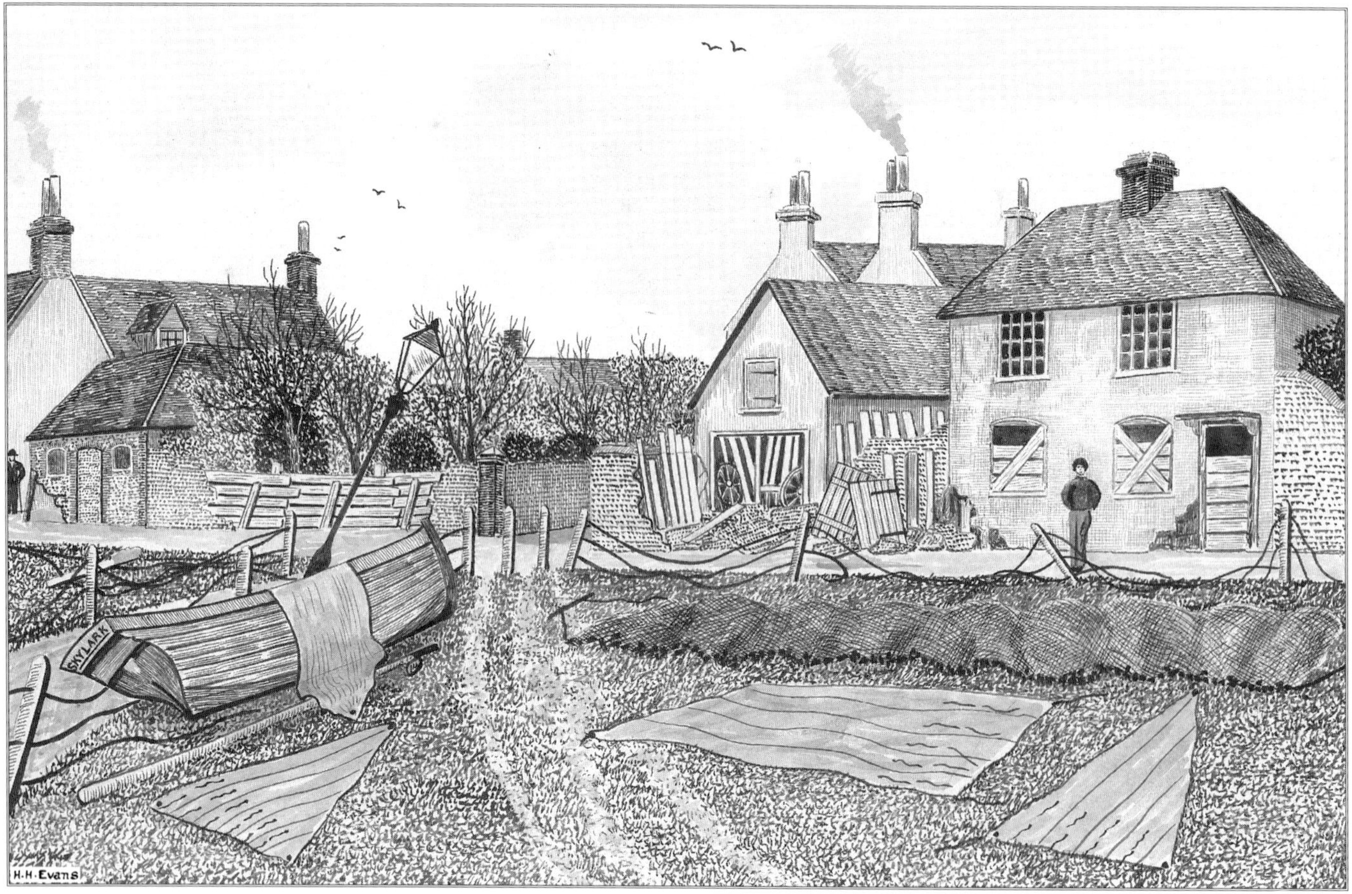

BOTTOM OF DARK LANE

COACH-HOUSE USED AS CARPENTERS SHOP AND OLD TILTMAN'S COTTAGE

AFTER THE FLOOD 1875.

Another view of the same scene showing how all Evans' drawings differed slightly even when recording similar events and places.

(Size of original drawing 165 x 210mm)

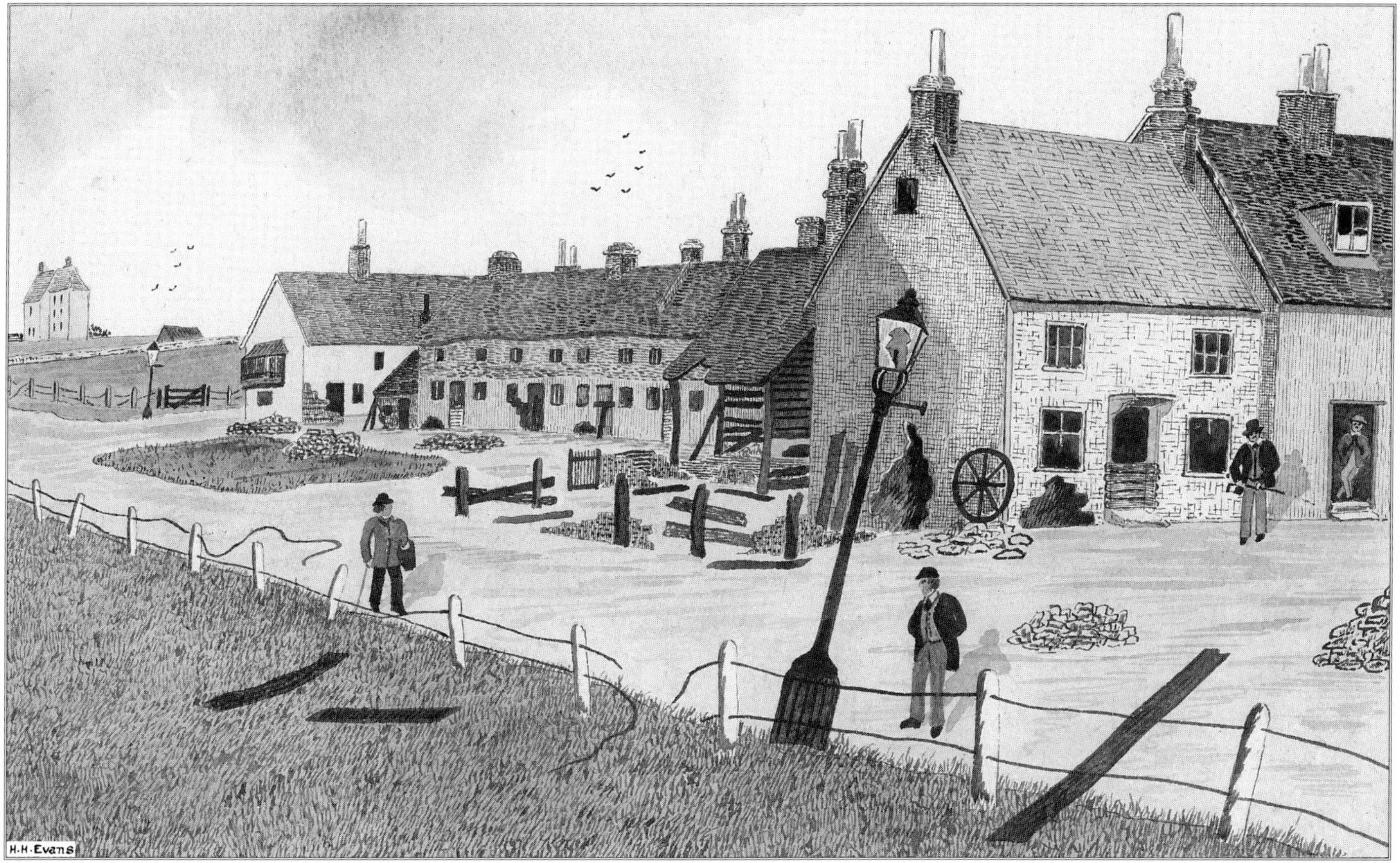

AFTER THE FLOOD, *LOOKING WEST.*

West House and Parliament Row.
(Size of original drawing 145 x 225mm)

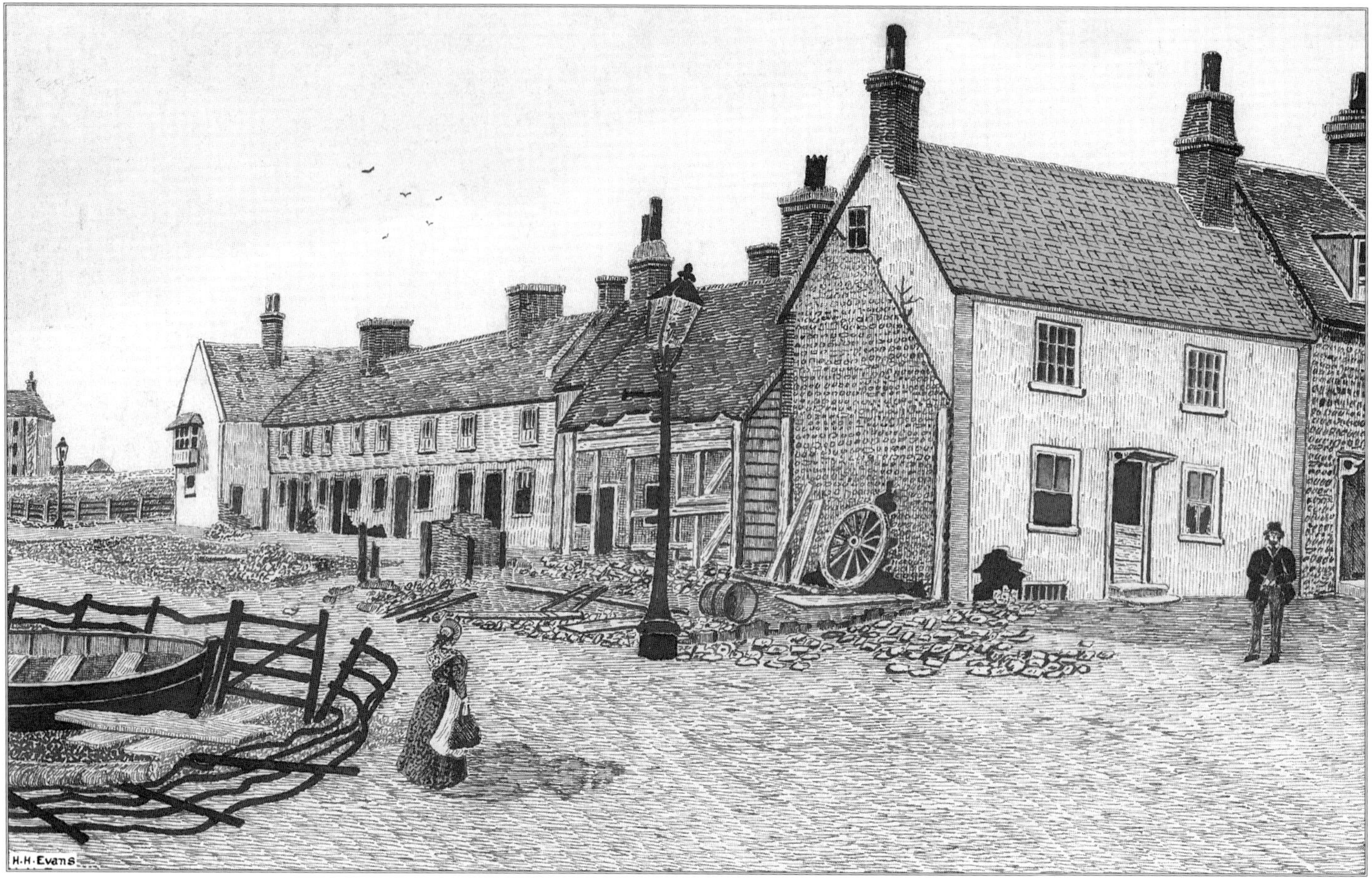

PARLIAMENT ROW, SEAFORD.
Damage, done by Flood 1875.

A similar view from another set of drawings. Note how the lamp post has moved position and the perspective has changed.
(Size of original drawing 150 x 205mm)

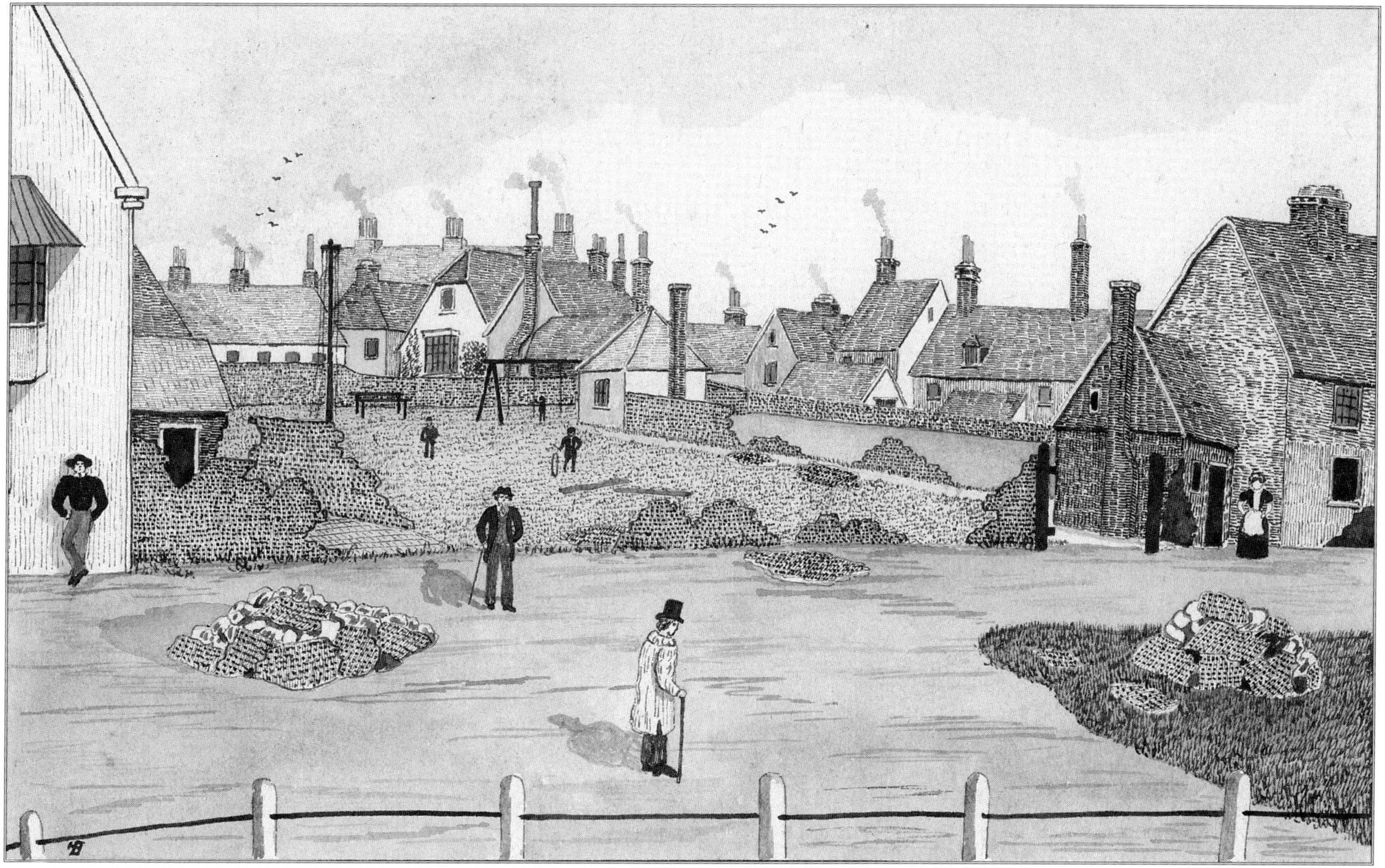

At the time of the flood, West House was a private school for young gentlemen.
(Size of original drawing 160 x 210mm)

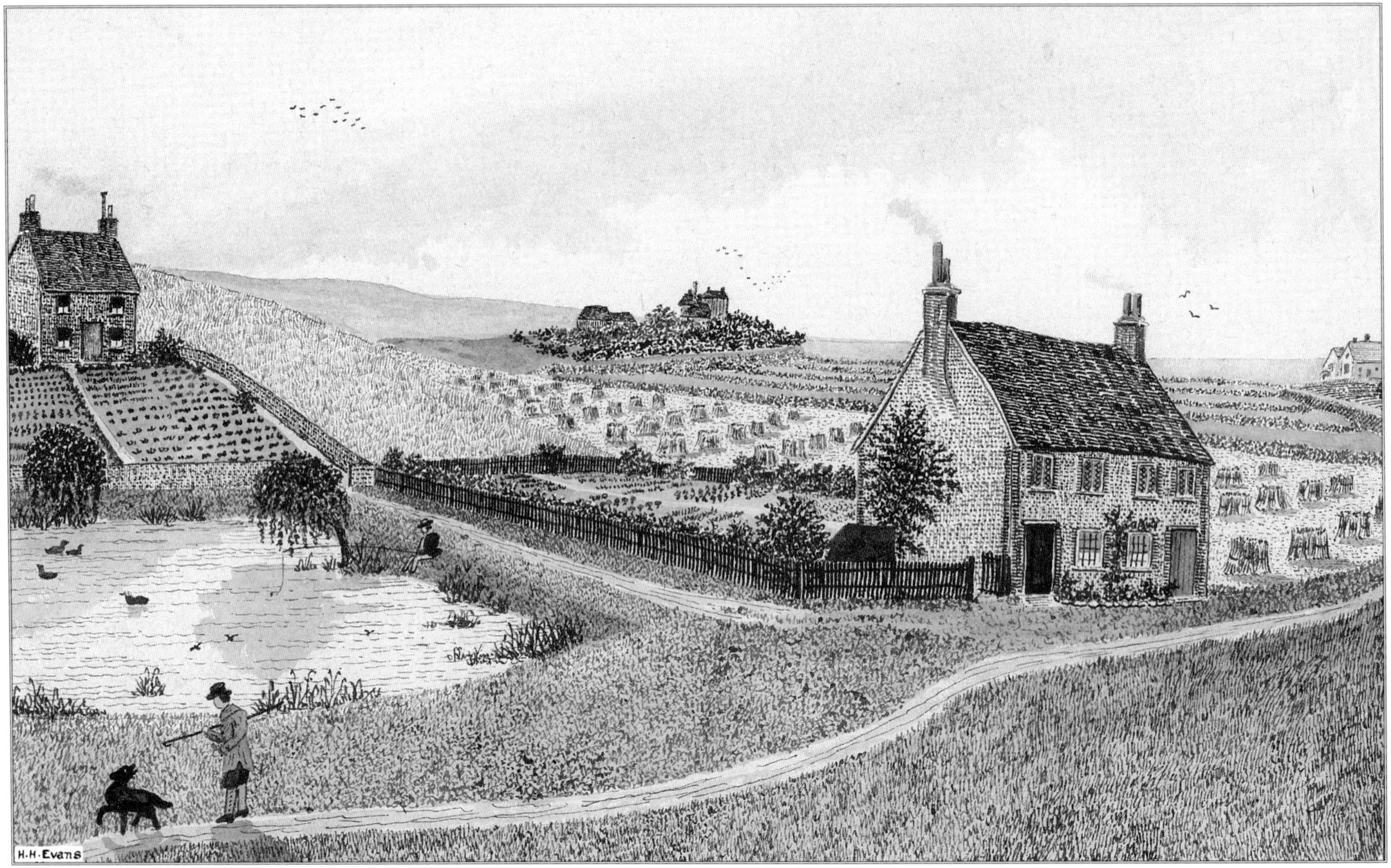

LIONS PLACE.

Cottages in foreground pulled down after Flood

The source of this drawing is not known at present and it is difficult to locate.

(Size of original drawing 155 x 210mm)

Ships and Shipwrecks

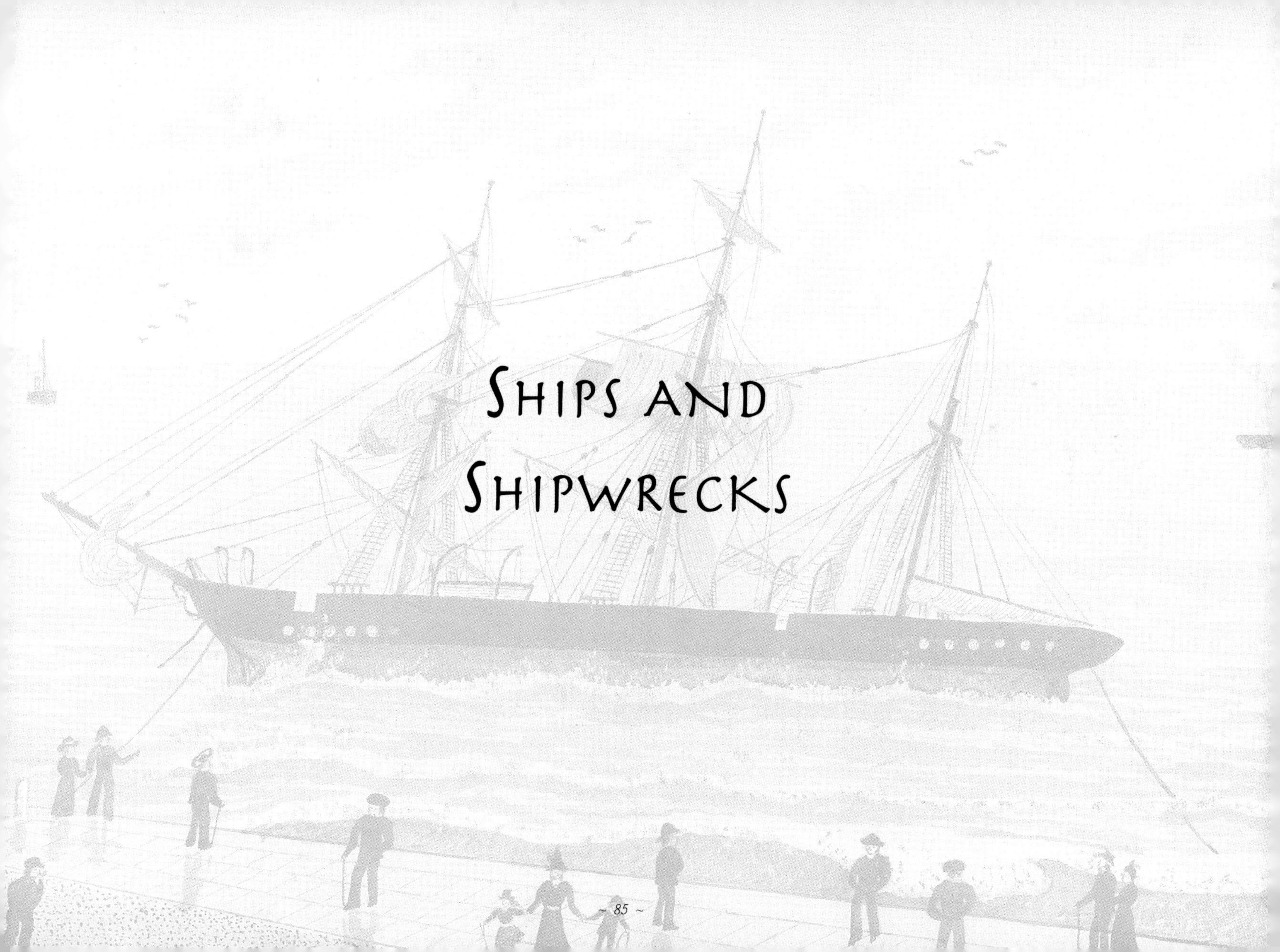

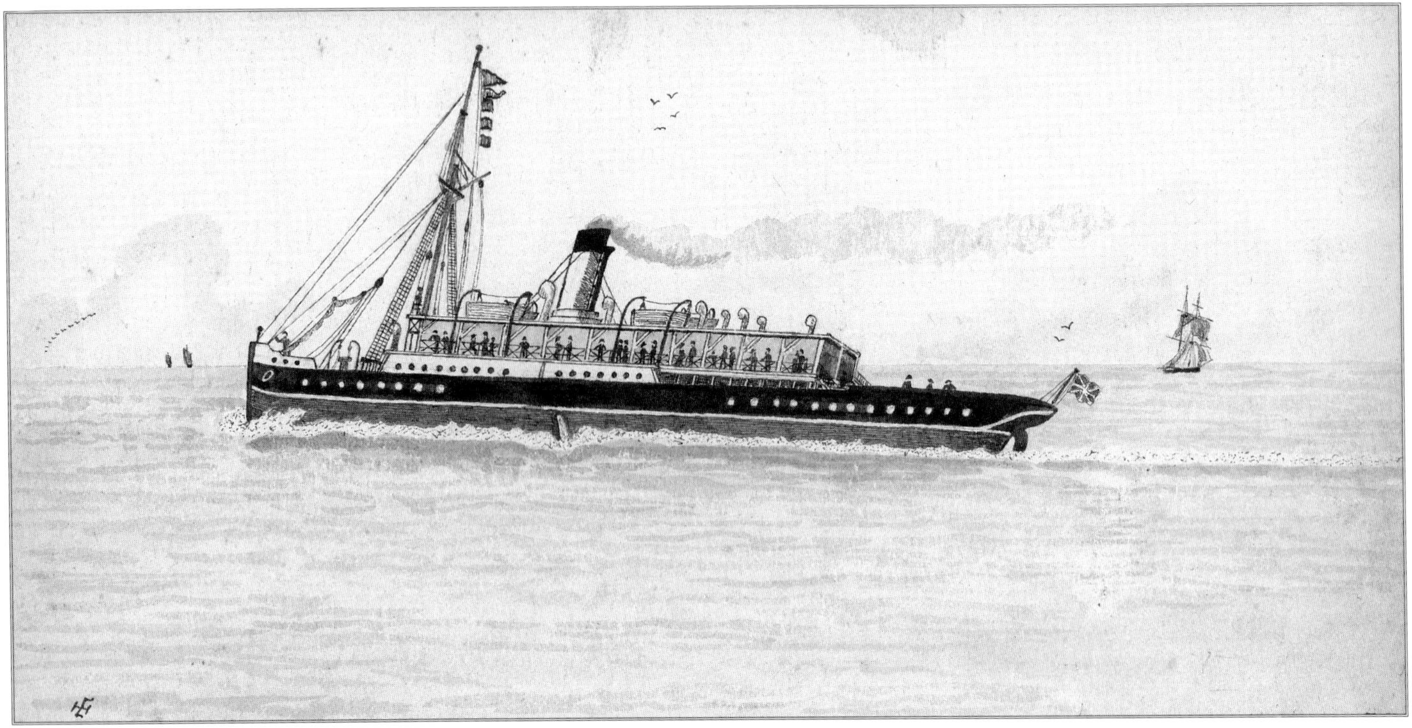

"SEAFORD"

Steel twin screw, 997 gr tons, 5000 horse power

Capt. Sharpe, — Ch. Eng. Moneypenny.

Sunk by S.S. Lyon, 25 miles off Beachy Head, in a fog, Augst. 22nd. 1895.

225 Passengers & 42 Crew saved,

by S.S. Lyon.

The *SS Seaford* which was lost in 1895. A teaspoon rescued by a survivor is in the Seaford Museum.
(Size of original drawing 170 x 280mm)

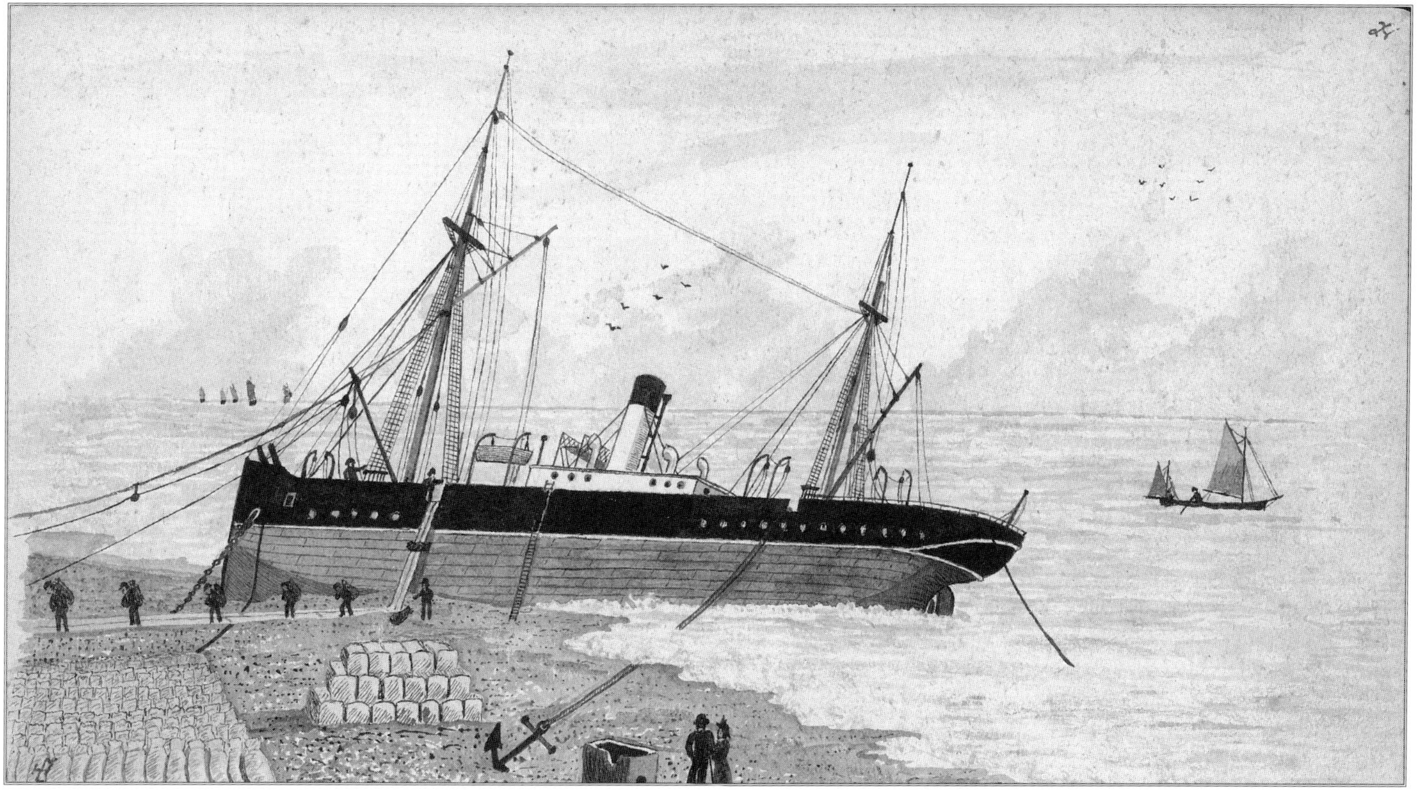

S. S. "GANNETT."

From Calcutta to London

Grounded in Seaford Bay 14th Feby 1882.

Captn J. Smith.

Passengers landed at Southampton.

Crew saved by Rocket Apparatus.

The *SS Gannett* grounded 1882. (Size of original drawing 170 x 280mm)

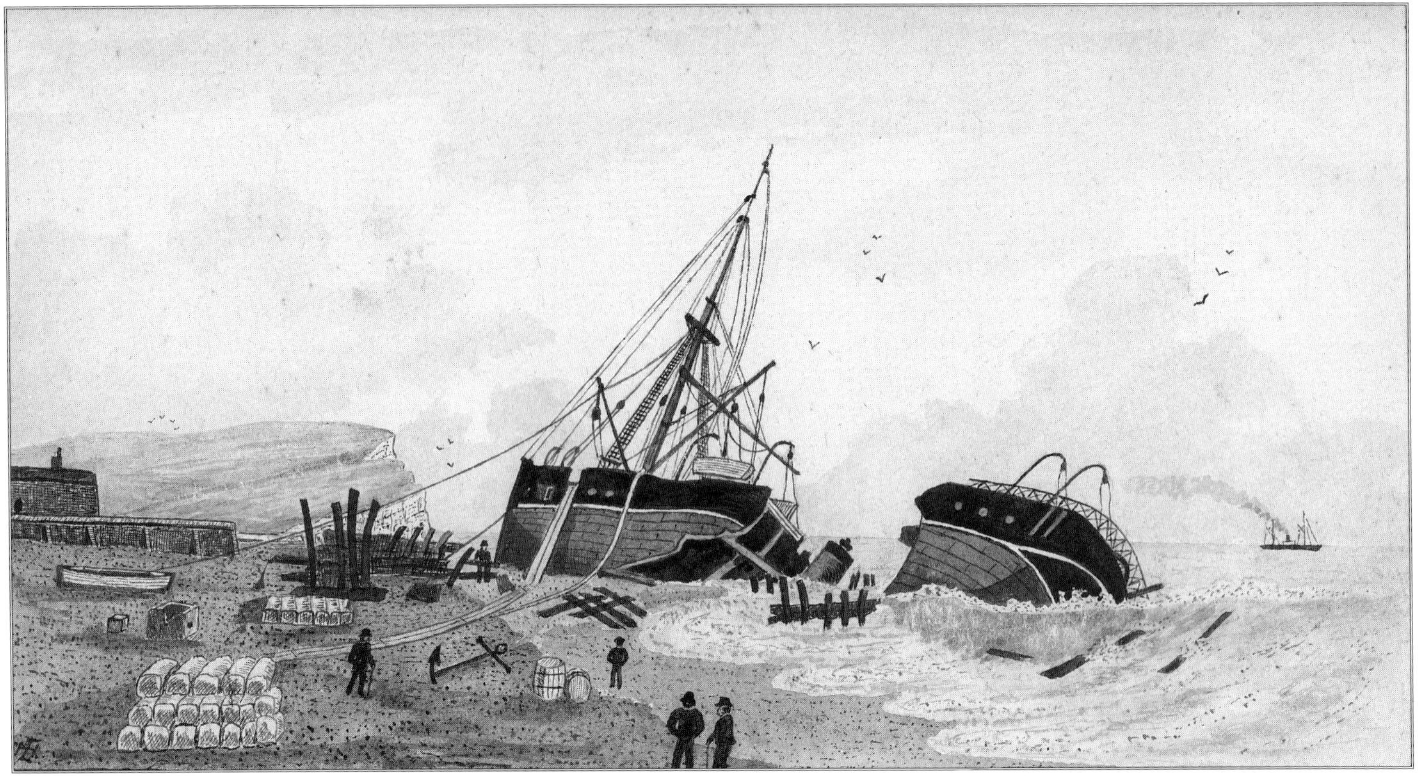

S. S. "GANNETT"

After the Gale on the 1st March.

CARGO

Tea, Coffee, Wheat, Rice,

Cotton, Indigo, Linseed.

Hides & Horns.

The *SS Gannett* breaking up. (Size of original drawing 170 x 260mm)

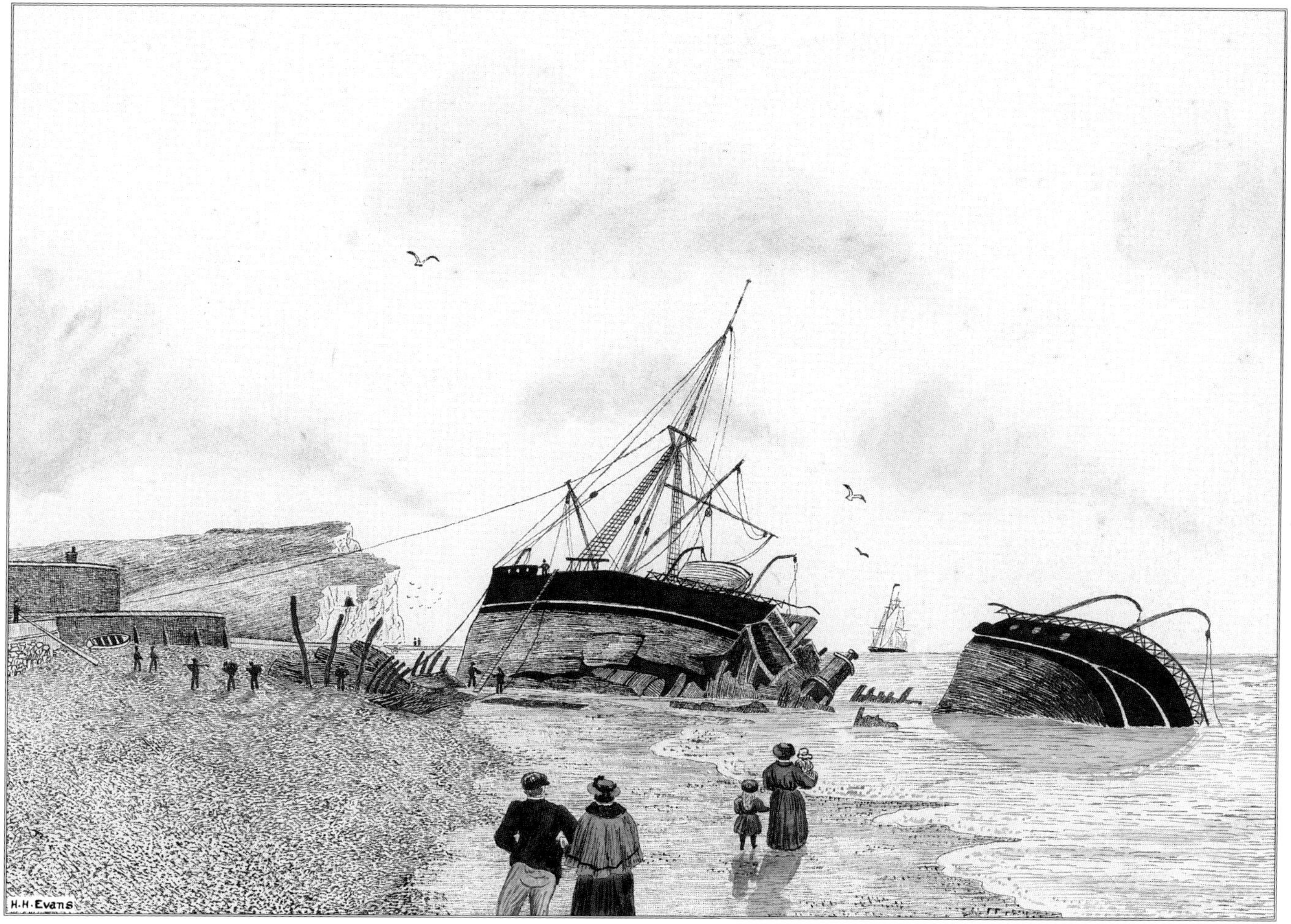

—< SEAFORD BEACH — LOOKING EAST. >—
— WRECK OF THE 'GANNET', FEBRUARY 14TH 1882. —

The wreck of the *SS Gannett* immediately below the Martello Tower. (Size of original drawing 160 x 210mm)

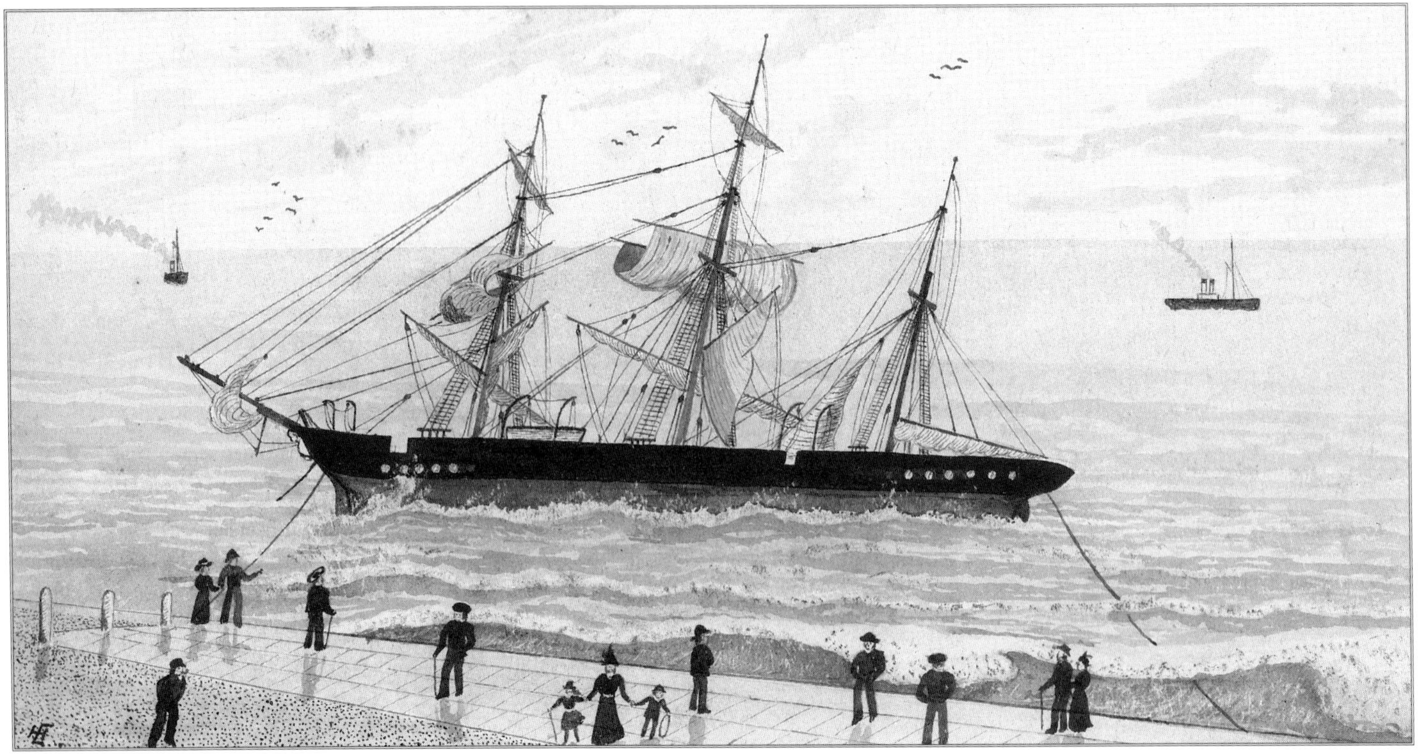

"PERUVIAN"

DANISH BARQUE.

Bound from Esmeralda to Hamburg.

Capt. Norholm – 149 days on voyage.

Life-boat "Michael Henry" saved the Captain and nine of the crew.

Second mate saved by rocket apparatus, First mate Neilson was drowned.

The wreck of the *Peruvian* 1899. The figurehead and some of the ivory nuts from the cargo are in Seaford Museum. The ivory nuts in the Museum, carrying pictures of the *Peruvian*, are thought also to be the work of Evans. (Size of original drawing 170 x 280mm)

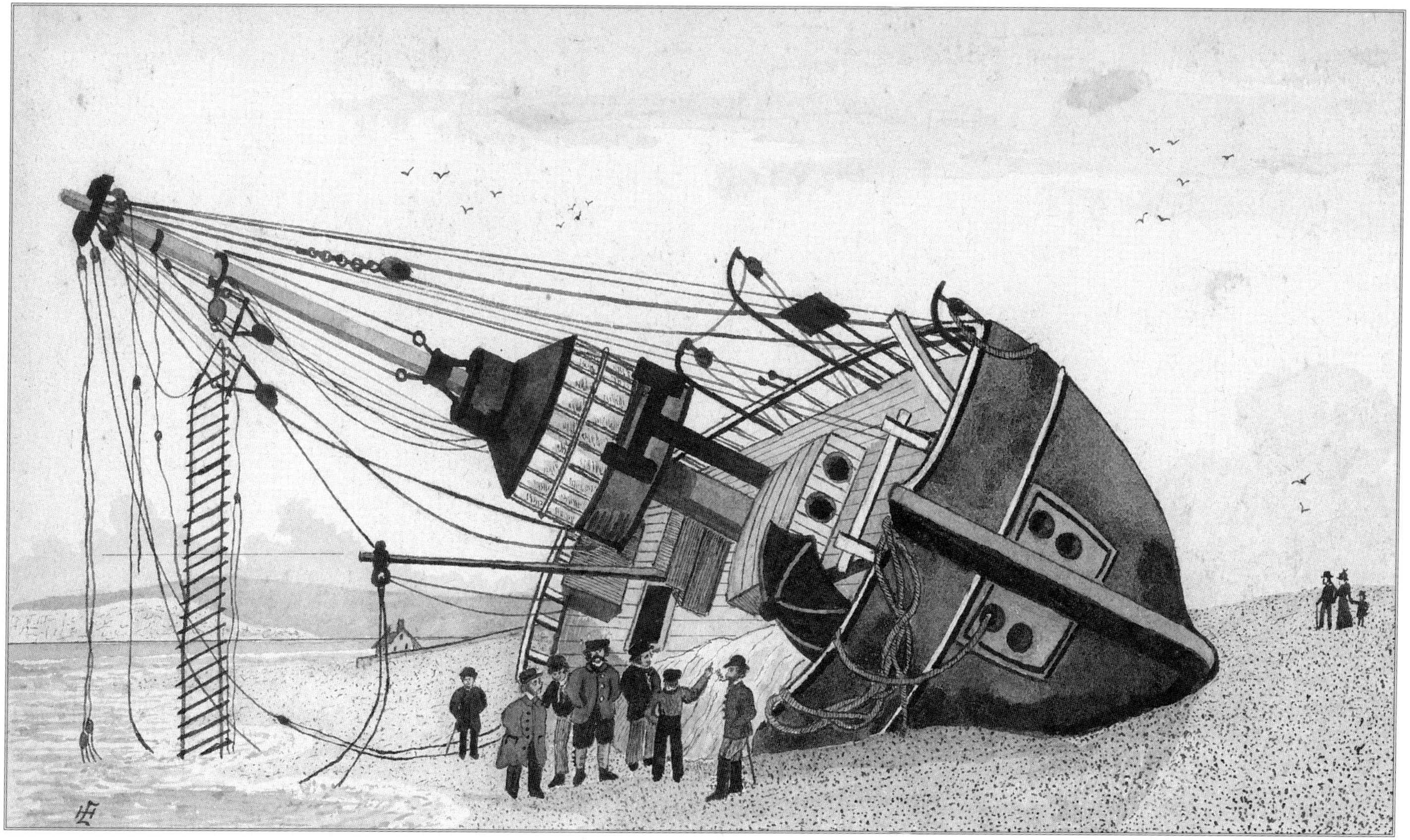

"WARNER" LIGHTSHIP.

Draged her, anchors, off Newhaven Breakwater,
and, drifted, ashore in a gale 21st Octr 1895.
one seaman drowned.

The *Warner* lightship ashore in 1895. (Size of original drawing 170 x 270mm)

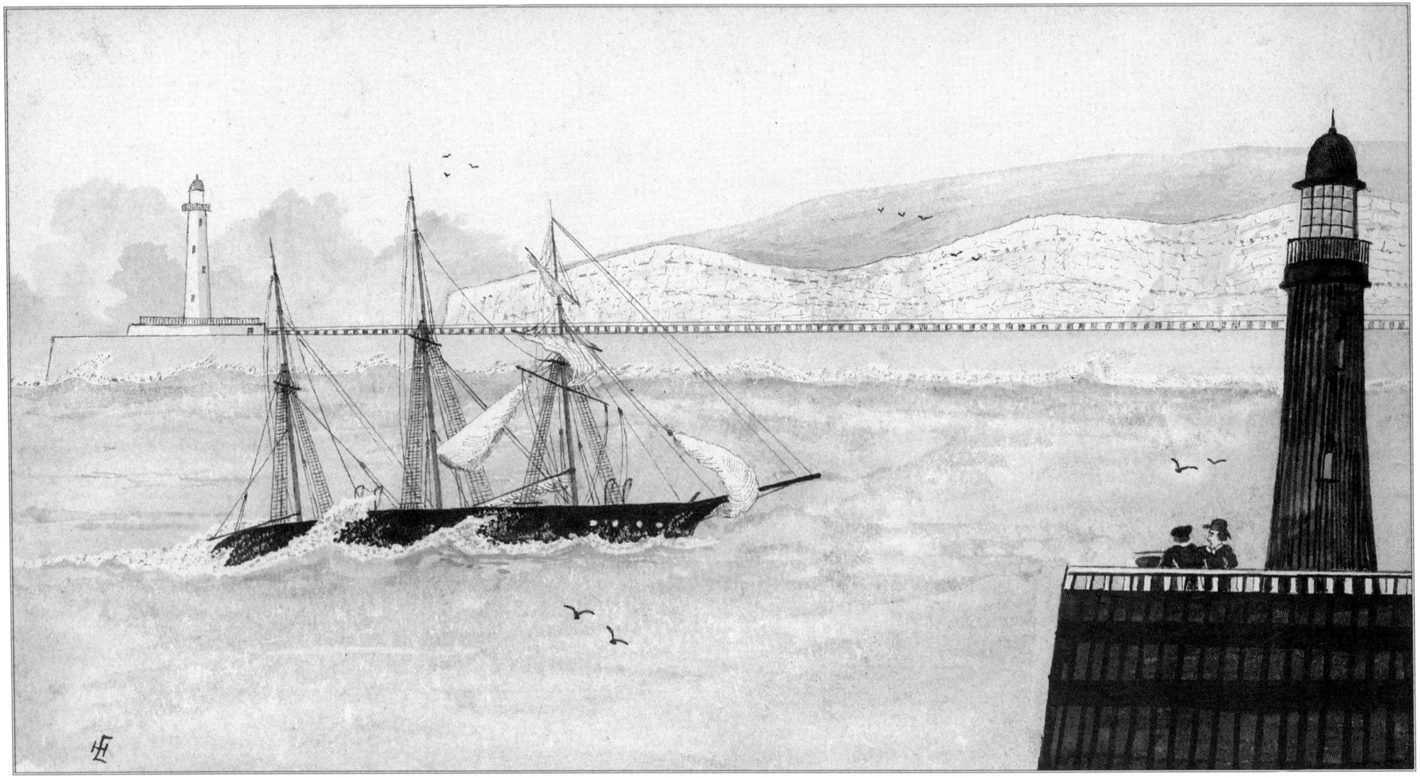

Brigatine "OREALA." of Guernsey.
from Cherbourg to Shoreham
200 tons reg.
Captn. Wright.
Grounded and became a total wreck under Newhaven Breakwater
22nd August 1899.
Cargo - Broken Granite - Crew saved.

The *Oreala* wrecked at Newhaven 1899. (Size of original drawing 180 x 270mm)

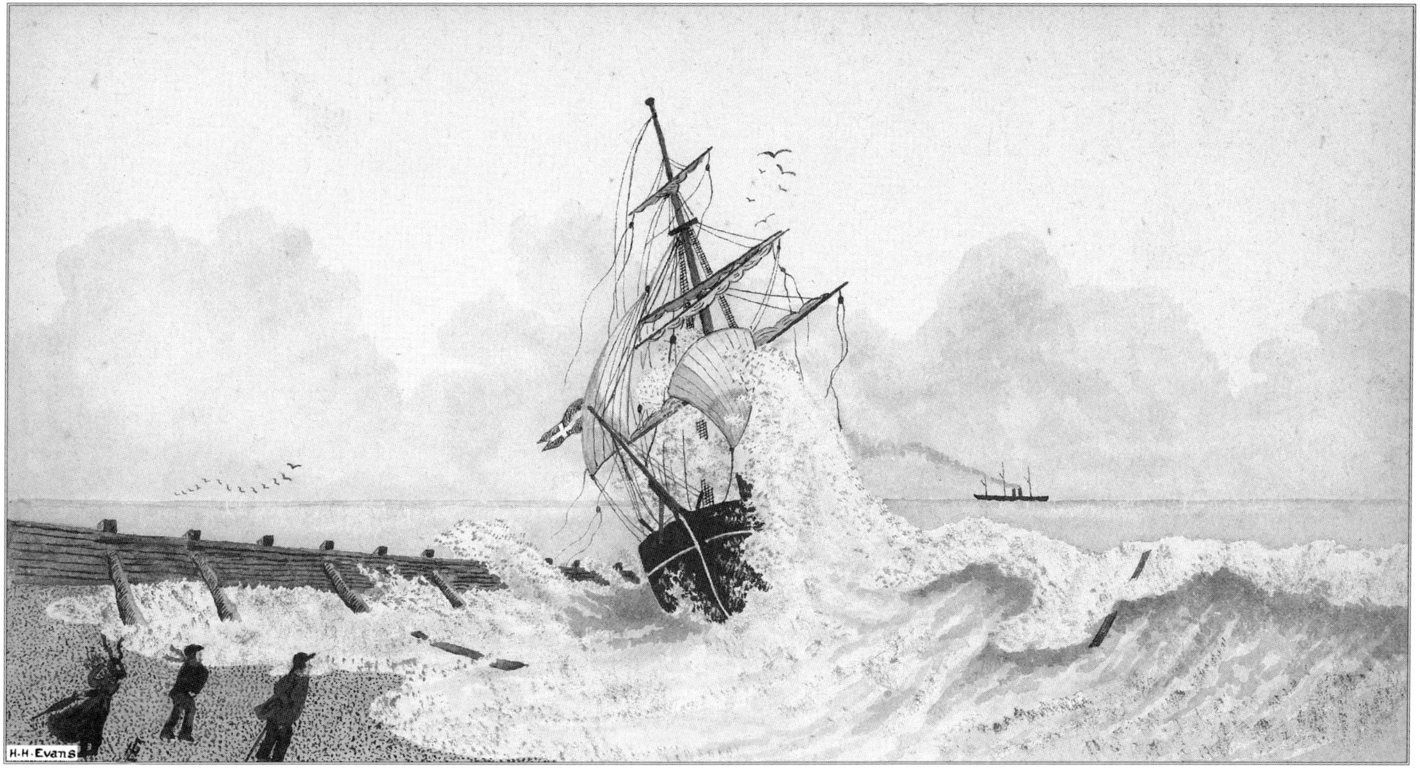

"SAGATUN."

NORWEGIAN BARQUE.

From Pitea to Newhaven.

Became a total wreck in Seaford Bay, 26th Sept. 1900.

Captn. Simensen & his daughter aged 15 yrs.,

and crew of 9 men – were saved by the Rocket apparatus.

The *Sagatun* wrecked in 1900. (Size of original drawing 175 x 270mm)

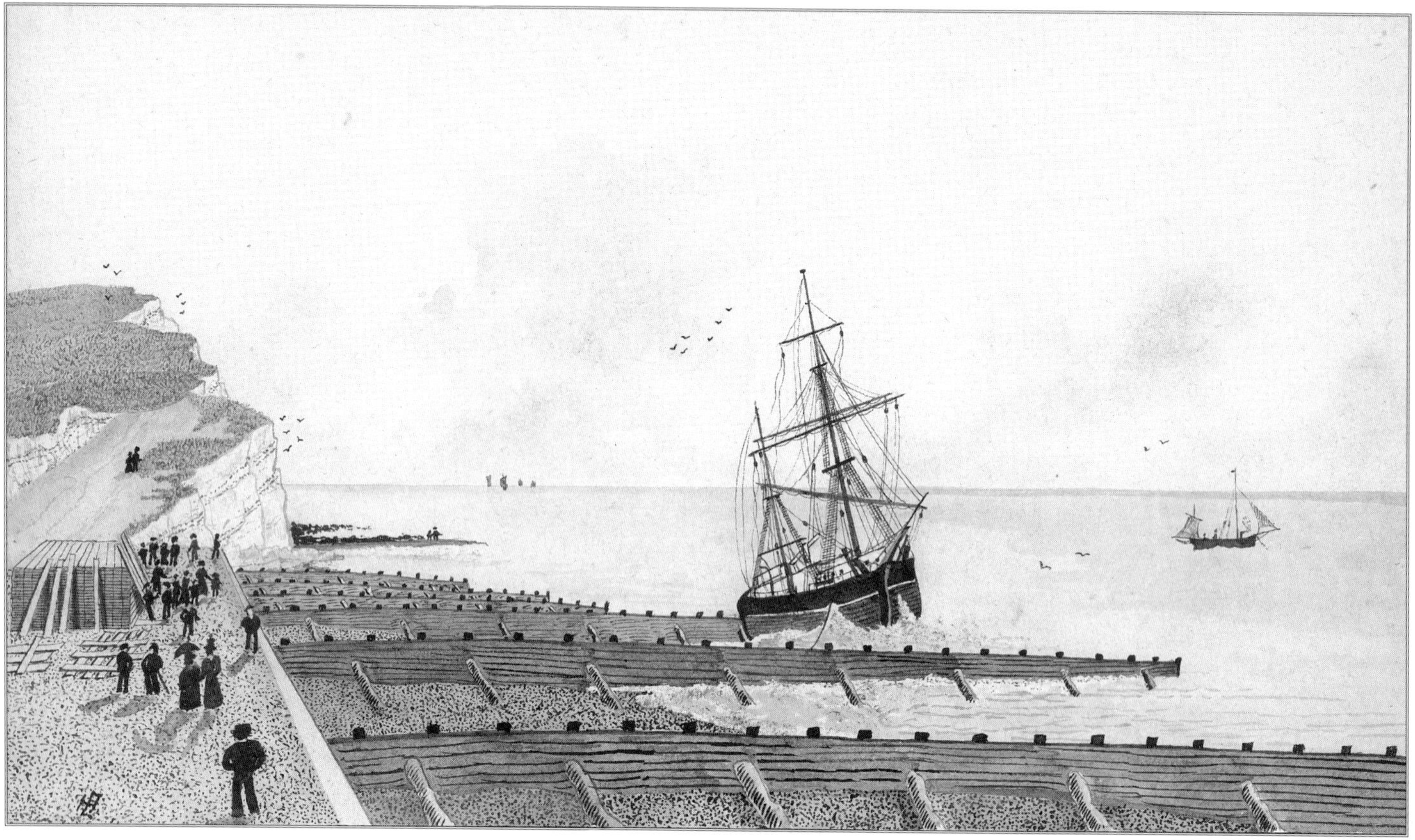

"SAGATUN."
500 tons register.
Cargo – Timber.

The *Sagatun* showing the timber saved from the cargo.
(Size of original drawing 175 x 275mm)

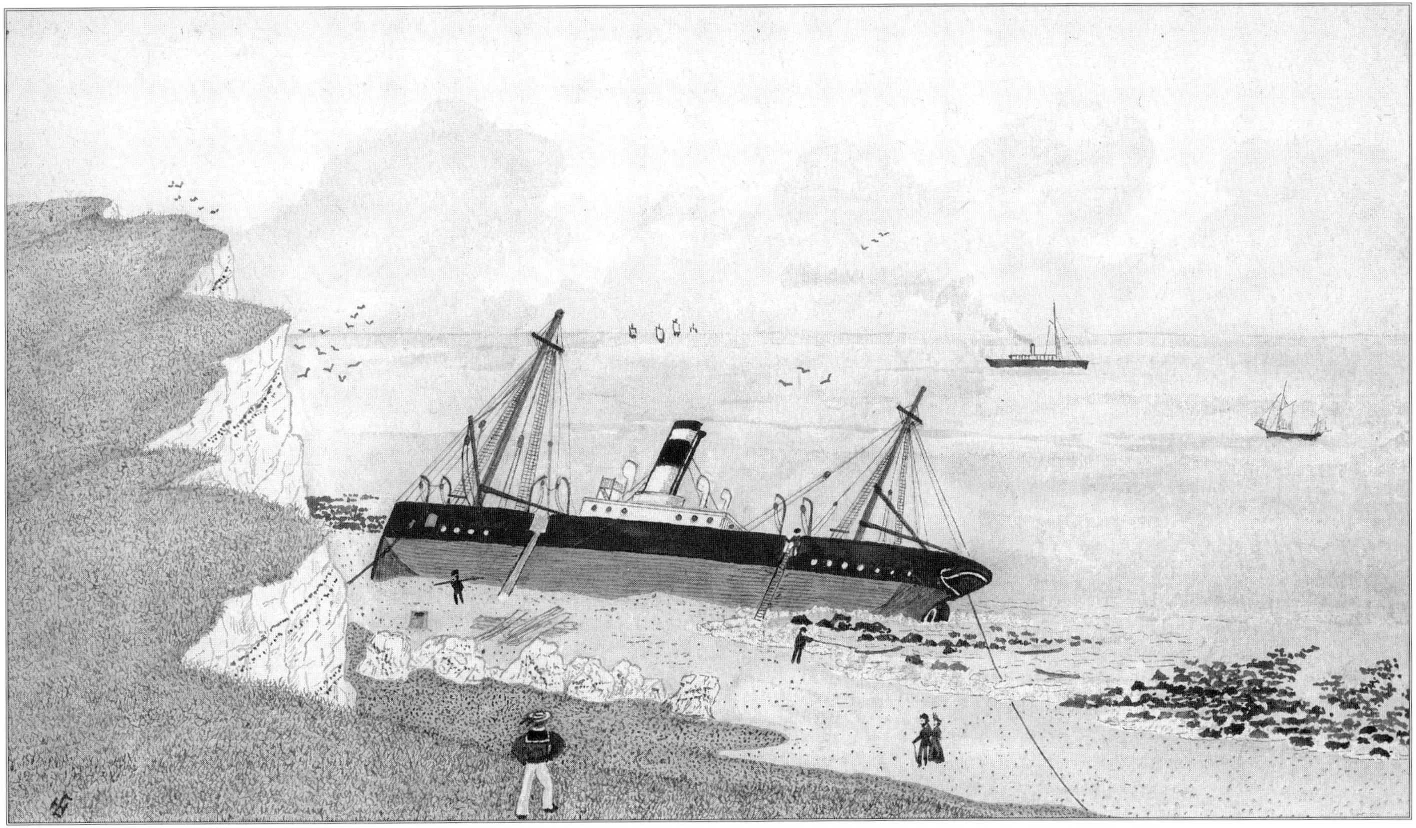

"INTERNATIONAL."

In Ballast.

Being towed up channel from Cherbourg to London, broke her hawser, and drifted ashore at Birling Gap, in a storm, on the 30th Aug. 1899.

Crew saved.

The *International* washed ashore at Birling Gap in 1899. (Size of original drawing 180 x 270mm)

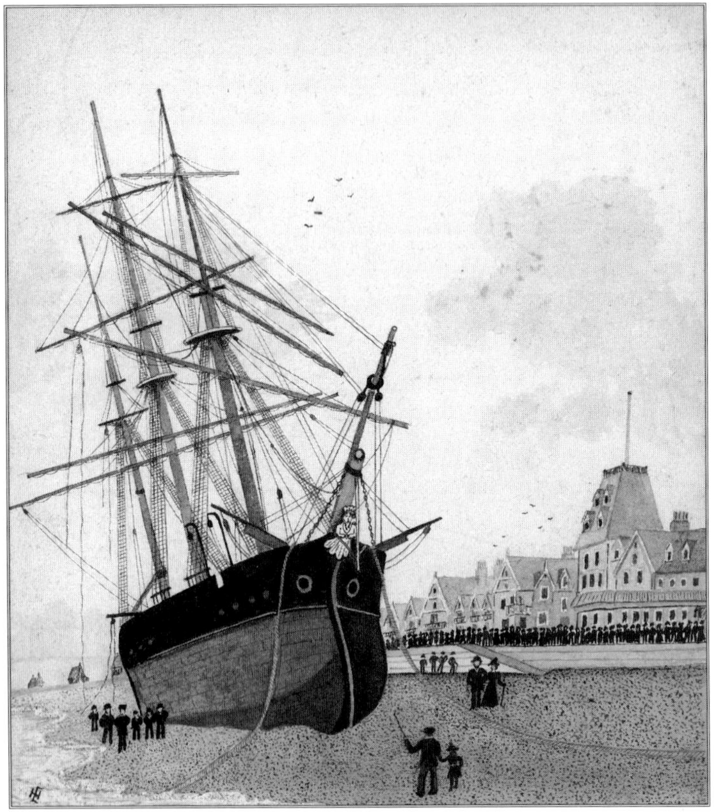

"PERUVIAN"

Driven ashore in a gale 8th Feby. 1899.

CARGO.

1,000 tons of Vegetable Ivory

and Logwood.

The *Peruvian* ashore opposite the Esplanade Hotel in 1899.
(Size of original drawing 245 x 185mm)

Seaford Museum

Seaford Museum is housed in Martello Tower 74 and its covered dry moat, which is situated at the eastern end of Seaford seafront. The Museum not only records Seaford's long and turbulent history but also appeals to all age groups and all members of the family with displays including shops, tableaux and a fascinating collection of material from pre-historic times to the present day.

The Museum has a reference archive of pictures, maps, texts etc. and a register of houses in the town. Both Archive and Housing Register are available for research by appointment or by letter or e-mail.

The Museum is without endowment and entirely run by the volunteer members of Seaford Museum and Heritage Society and therefore cost-covering donations are requested for research services.

Copies, in their original size, of drawings in the book are also available from the Museum shop (with the exception of those not in the Museum collection namely nos. 4, 15, 17, 47, 48, 49, 50).